Match Mine
Primary

Authors
Melissa Wincel
Laurie Kagan

Concept and Development
Miguel Kagan

Illustrations
Erin Kant
Ally MacWilliams

Publisher
Kagan Publishing

Kagan

Kagan Publishing
981 Calle Amanecer
San Clemente, CA 92673
1 (800) 933-2667
www.KaganOnline.com

ISBN: 978-1-933445-36-6

Table of Contents

30 Match Mine Games!

Game

How to Play

Match Mine

Partners must communicate with precision in order for the Receiver to match the Sender's arrangement of game pieces on a game board.

> At the Primary grades, Match Mine can be played four different ways, depending on your students' level and experience. Level 1 is the easiest, and level 4 is the most difficult. Start at level 1 and work your way up to level 4.

Level 1

Side by Side Without Barrier

Students pair up. Partners sit side by side (shoulder partners) without a barrier. They each have an identical game board and game pieces. Game pieces may be identical or may match based on the concept skill. Partner A is the "Sender" and Partner B is the "Receiver." To start, Sender sends one direction at a time, telling Receiver to find a specific game piece. Once found, Receiver gives Sender a thumbs up. Sender then tells Receiver where to place that game piece. Receiver places game piece and says, *"Ready for the next piece."* At this beginning level, limit the number of game pieces to three or four. The object of the game is for Sender and Receiver to communicate clearly so Receiver can perfectly match Sender's arrangement. Receiver listens carefully and follows Sender's directions. When done, Sender and Receiver switch roles.

Level 2

Side by Side With Barrier

Students pair up. Partners sit side by side (shoulder partners) with a barrier between them, so they can't see each other's game board. They each have an identical game board and game pieces. Game pieces may be identical or may match based on the concept skill. Partner A is the "Sender" and Partner B is the "Receiver." To start, Sender sends one direction at a a time, telling Receiver to find a specific game piece. Once found, Receiver gives Sender a thumbs up. Sender then tells Receiver where to place that game piece. Receiver places game piece and says, *"Ready for the next piece."* At this beginning level, limit the number of game pieces to four or five. The object of the game is for Sender and Receiver to communicate clearly so Receiver can perfectly match Sender's arrangement. Receiver listens carefully and follows Sender's directions, asking clarifying questions if needed. Sender and Receiver remove barrier and compare boards, praising for the clear directions and giving coaching tips for clearer directions if necessary. When done, Sender and Receiver switch roles.

Level 3

Face to Face, Build it Together

Students pair up. Partners sit face to face (face partners) with a barrier between them, so they can't see each other's game board. They each have an identical game board and game pieces. Game pieces may be identical or may match based on the concept skill. Partner A is the "Sender" and Partner B is the "Receiver." To start, Sender sends one direction at a time, telling Receiver to find a specific game piece. Once found, Receiver gives Sender a thumbs up. Sender then tells Receiver where to place that game piece. Receiver places game piece and says, *"I'm ready for the next piece."* At this level, limit the number of game pieces to six to eight. The object of the game is for Sender and Receiver to communicate clearly so Receiver can perfectly match Sender's arrangement. Receiver listens carefully and follows Sender's directions, asking clarifying questions if needed. When all game pieces have been placed, the barrier is removed and boards are placed side by side to see if their game boards match. Receiver praises for the clear directions and gives coaching tips for clearer directions if necessary. When done, Sender and Receiver switch roles.

Level 4

Face to Face

Students pair up. Partners sit face to face (face partners) with a barrier between them, so they can't see each other's game board. They each have an identical game board and game pieces. Game pieces may be identical or may match based on the concept skill. Partner A is the "Sender" and Partner B is the "Receiver." To start, Sender sets up his game board while Receiver waits patiently and quietly. Set a time limit for the game board set up, 30–45 seconds. Sender lays out all of his or her game pieces on the game board in any arrangement without talking to Receiver. Sender cannot move the game pieces once they are all set in one place. The object of the game is for Sender and Receiver to communicate clearly so Receiver can perfectly match Sender's arrangment. To make a match, Sender describes his or her arrangement by explaining the location of each game piece. Receiver listens carefully and follows Sender's directions. Once all directions are sent, the barrier is removed and boards are placed side by side to see if their game boards match. Receiver praises and together they brainstorm tips for game piece placements that don't match. When done, Sender and Receiver switch roles.

Getting Ready

Students pair up. One is the Sender, the other is the Receiver. Each partner receives an identical game board and either identical game pieces or game pieces that match based on the concept. For level 1, partners sit side by side. For Level 2, they sit side by side with a barrier in between. For Level 3 and Level 4, Sender and Receiver sit on opposite sides of a barrier.

For Level 1-3 Steps

1. Game Board and Game Pieces

The Sender and the Receiver lay out game pieces next to their game board. For Level 1 and Level 2, limit the game pieces to 3 or 4 game pieces. For Level 3, limit game pieces to 6 to 8 game pieces.

2. Sender Directs Receiver

The Sender gives the Receiver a direction to find a specific game piece. Once that game piece is found, Receiver gives Sender a thumbs up. Sender then tells Receiver where to place that game piece on the game board. Receiver then says, *"I'm ready for the next piece."* Sender continues to send directions one game piece at a time until all game pieces are placed.

Instructions may sound like, *"Find the picture that begins with the /a/ sound. Place the /a/ picture at the top of the beehive."*

3. Partners Check

Once all game pieces have been placed, partners check to see if their game boards match. For Level 3, partners carefully set their game boards side by side to check for accuracy, *"OK, it sounds like we have a match; let's check."*

4. Praise and Plan

The Receiver praises the Sender for his or her instructions and they develop improvement strategies. *"Great Job! Next time, it would be helpful if you said which row of the beehive."*

5. Switch Roles

The Receiver now becomes the Sender and Sender becomes Receiver. The pair plays again.

Match Mine

Match Mine: Primary
Kagan Publishing • 1 (800) 933-2667 • www.KaganOnline.com

Match Mine

Directions: Enlarge to poster size. Use as a visual reference for students to see while doing the Match Mine structure.

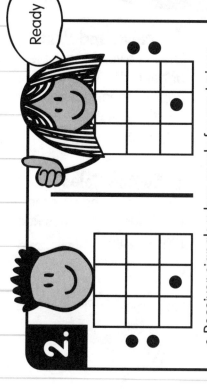

1. Place it...
- Sender gives direction
- Receiver places game piece

2. Ready
- Receiver signals when ready for next piece
- Continue until done

3. Great job!
- Compare arrangements
- Sender prasies Receiver or provides tips

4. Place it...
- Sender and Reciever switch roles
- Play again

Level 4 Steps

1. Sender Creates Arrangement
The Sender arranges his or her game pieces on his or her game board while the Receiver waits patiently and quietly. Set a time limit of 30 seconds to set up the game pieces on the game board. Limit the game pieces to 8 to 12 game pieces.

2. Sender Directs Receiver
The Sender gives the Receiver directions to match Sender's arrangement of game pieces on the game board. Instructions may sound like, *"Put the letter Bb in the fourth row, first box."* Receiver gives Sender a thumbs up and says, *"I'm ready for the next piece."*

3. Partners Check
When finished, partners carefully set their game boards side by side to check for accuracy. *"OK, it sounds like we have a matc; let's check."*

4. Praise and Plan
The Receiver praises the Sender for his or her instructions and they develop improvement strategies. *"Great Job! Next time, it would be helpful if you said which row of the beehive."*

5. Switch Roles
The Receiver now becomes the Sender and Sender becomes Receiver. The pair plays again.

Match Mine

Match Mine: Primary
Kagan Publishing • 1 (800) 933-2667 • www.KaganOnline.com

Introduction

Why Play Match Mine?

The games in this book are specifically designed to build language skills, vocabulary, and practice skills outlined in the Common Core State Standards (CCSS). They are ideal for students learning English as a second language and for little ones developing their native language skills. In addition, Match Mine is a fun format, yielding many important learning benefits for students:

• Develops academic vocabulary
• Improves verbal communication
• Enhances ability to give clear, concise directions
• Promotes active listening
• Nurtures cooperative skills
• Promotes role-taking ability
• Develops visual analysis
• Increases spatial and positional word vocabulary

Management Modifications

• Add color dots, shapes, letters, or numbers on game boards if students aren't at the level where they can give clear, concise positional word directions. Once that skill has been taught, remove the colors, shapes, letters, or numbers from the game boards.

Successful Implementation

• Whole Group Activity

The teacher is the Sender; the whole Class is the Receiver. Each student has a game board and game pieces.

• Small Group Instruction

During your guided reading or math, use Match Mine to practice a specific skill you are focusing on. Each pair of students receives a Match Mine game set. You want to eavesdrop on the directions the Sender gives, intervening to coach on giving more clear, concise directions. When students are successful at this level, you are ready to move Match Mine to an independent learning center.

• Learning Center

Match Mine can be done at a center. At a center, you may have two of the same games set up to accommodate four students. This is a great structures that allows you to differentiate based on your students ability levels. Color coding game boards will aid in this differentiation.

• Sponge Activity

Match Mine is a great activity students can play when they've finished their work.

• Whole Class Activity

The whole class can play Match Mine at the same time. Each pair receives a Match Mine game set.

What's in This Book?

Intro Page

For each of the 30 games in this book, you will find an introduction page that shows the game board and game pieces, and lists the vocabulary that game develops. Relevant Common Core State Standards are listed.

Game Board

Each of the 30 games has a unique game board. The game board is a reproducible page. Make 1 copy of the game board for each student playing (2 game boards per pair).

Game Pieces

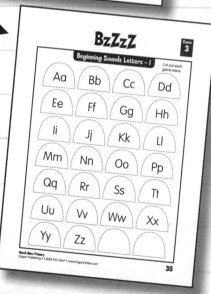

There are game pieces for Partner A and Partner B. For some games, they are identical; for others, they are matching skill sets. If they fit, the game pieces for both partners are on the same page. Otherwise, the game pieces are on two pages, one set per page. Make a copy of the game pieces so each student has a set. Limit the number of pieces based on the skills you are focusing on. Place those game pieces in individual resealable bags for each partner.

Playing Tips

Sponge Activity

Pairs will finish at different rates. When they're done, let them play a different Match Mine game or play the same game using a variation described on pages 14–15.

Creating a Barrier

A barrier is set up between each pair. The preferred barrier is a file folder barrier that is cut so that it is at chin level of your students. This will reduce the noise level as their voices will not be reverberating back on the file folder. To make a file folder barrier, you will need two file folders and a paper clip. Place the file folders back to back, and paper clip the top of the file folders together as illustrated. Next, open the file folders and spread out the bases so the barrier is self-standing. Instead of a paper clip, you can use staples or tape to keep the file folder together, but the paper clip doubles for a storage closure.

Alternative Barriers

Any barrier will work as long as students can hear each other but can't see each other's game board or game pieces. Alternate barrier options include the following:

- Pizza boxes
- Folders
- Binders
- Large books

Color Cardstock Paper

Copy the game board and game pieces on different colored paper. Cardstock is preferable if available because it makes the game more durable for re-use. Having a different colored game board and game pieces make the game pieces easier to see and easier to differentiate.

Laminate Games

For extra durability, laminate the game board and game pieces. Laminate the game pieces before they are cut out.

Model It

To introduce Match Mine to the class, model it using your document camera/overhead, or role-play.

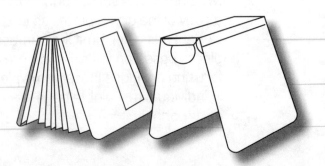

Match Mine: Primary
Kagan Publishing • 1 (800) 933-2667 • www.KaganOnline.com

Document Camera/Overhead Method: Provide each student with a game board and game pieces. Copy the game board and game pieces. If using an overhead, copy the game board and game pieces onto a sheet of transparency film. Game pieces should be copied on colored film if possible. When you model, set your game pieces on your game board so that your students cannot see your board. Then send directions one piece at a time to your Receivers (the whole class). Make sure to send bad directions, as well as good ones, so that students can see how important it is to send clear, concise directions. Each student builds his or her own game board. When it is time to check how well the students have matched your arrangement, turn on your document camera or overhead.

Role-Play Method: You role-play with another student. The student is the Sender and you are the Receiver. Purposely misinterpret vague directions. For example: If the student says, *"Place the circle on top of the square,"* you place the circle directly over the square, covering it up! The student meant above the square. If there is any ambiguity in the student's instructions, intentionally "go wrong" to demonstrate the importance of precise directions.

Do the Walkabout

As students play in pairs, walk around and eavesdrop on them. This is a great time to make corrections. If you notice similar problems, stop the class and make an adjustment.

Checking for Accuracy

When students think they made a match, they check for accuracy. The best way to check is for the Receiver to carefully move his or her game board side by side with the Sender's game board. Then, they check each game piece and pat each other on the back or do some celebration for each correct piece. If they are not side by side and do not check each piece, they may think they have made a match when in fact they haven't.

Processing Errors

If students find an error, they discuss why they made an error. Was the wrong vocabulary used? Was a direction not followed or interpreted correctly? Students find where they made a mistake and discuss how they can communicate more clearly next time.

Match Mine

Variations

Single Sender

Match Mine can be played as a whole class with a single Sender. The Sender can be the teacher or one student. The rest of the class are the Receivers. Sender (at the overhead) builds an arrangement and describes it to the whole class. Receivers follow Sender's instructions. Because the whole-class format cuts down on active participation, it is suggested only for younger students or for initial demonstrations.

Teams of Four

Match Mine may also be played in teams. Each team is provided two sets of game pieces, two game boards, and one barrier. Pairs are seated on each side of the barrier with their game board and game pieces. One pair is designated as Senders, the other as Receivers. For equal participation, the two Senders alternate giving instructions. Receivers discuss placing the game pieces and alternate placing them.

Build What I Write

Partners are sitting across from each other with a barrier in between. Each student gets two sets of manipulatives and two gameboards (e.g., pattern blocks, tangrams, geoboard, toothpicks, Legos, or blocks). Each partner builds a creation on one gameboard. You may want to limit pieces based on their transitional word fluency: first, next, then, finally. On a blank piece of writing paper, each partner writes the directions for their partner to build their creation based on their written directions. Students then switch instructions. Students use the written description to try to make a match. When they think they are correct, they remove the barrier and compare their creations with their partners.

Silent Partner

To add a degree of difficulty, introduce a fun variation called, "Silent Partner." In this variation, only the Sender is allowed to speak. The Receiver cannot ask for clarification during the game. This requires precise instructions and active listening.

Yes or No

Yes or No borrows from the game 20 Questions. The Sender builds an arrangement. When done, the Receiver tries to match the layout. As in the game 20 Questions, Reciever may only ask Sender "Yes" or "No" questions.

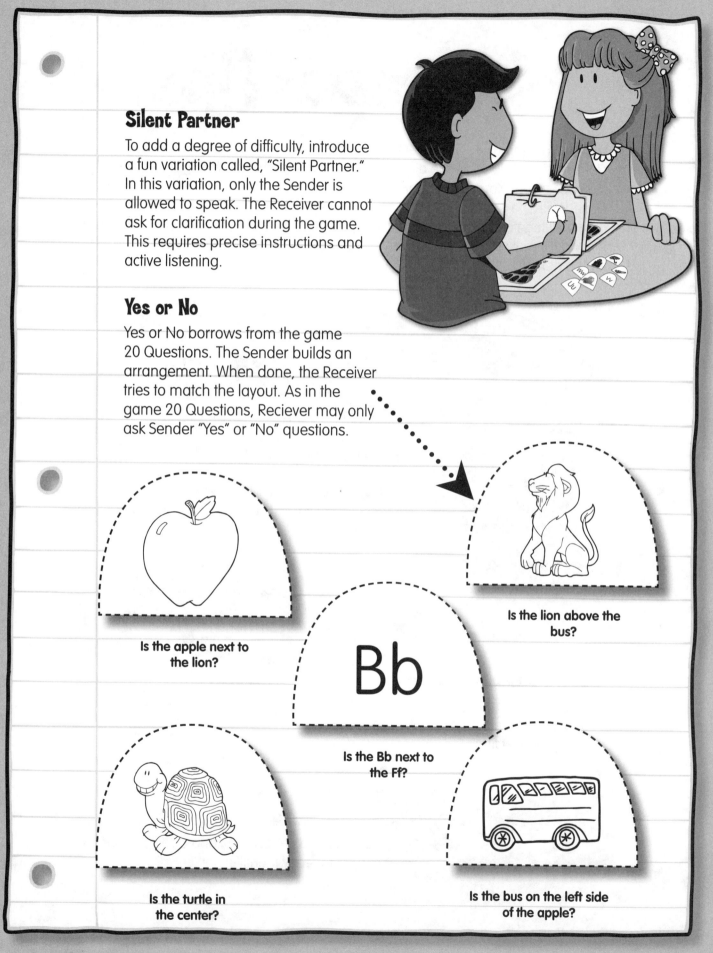

Is the apple next to the lion?

Is the lion above the bus?

Bb

Is the Bb next to the Ff?

Is the turtle in the center?

Is the bus on the left side of the apple?

Storage Tips

We recommend using file folders as barriers because they fold flat, ideal for storage. When students are done playing, have them place their game pieces in separate envelopes or resealable sandwich bags. Then, they fold the barriers closed with the game board and game piece bags inside and use the paper clip to hold it all together. Store the class set together. If you store your Match Mine games this way, it makes it quick and easy to pass out the games and set them up again for the next use.

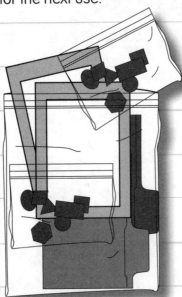

Store Each Game Separately

- Place game pieces in two separate resealable, plastic sandwich bags or envelopes
- Fold game boards into file folders
- Paper clip the set together
- Insert the entire set into a large, resealable plastic bag or catalog envelope

Store Games Together

Keep all the same games together and label the class set so they are ready for next time!

Match Mine Shapes

- Alternative storage option: Place entire set in a pizza box and add a picture label for easy identification.

Apples Up on Top

Partner A reads a sight word to Partner B. Partner B finds the same sight word and places it on the Apples Up on Top game board. Partner B cooperates with Partner A to make a match.

Game Board

Apples Up on Top
Game 1

Game Pieces

Apples Up on Top
Dolch Preprimer – 1   Cut out each game piece.

| a | and | away | big |
| blue | | come | down |

Differentiation

Depending on the reading level of your students, you can customize Dolch sight word sets that are appropriate for your student pairs. Sight word pieces include Preprimer, Primer, Grade One, and Grade Two, focusing on students' zone of proximal development.

Vocabulary

- A
- After
- Again
- All
- Always
- Am
- An
- And
- Any
- Apple
- Are
- Around
- As
- Ask
- At
- Ate
- Away
- Be
- Because
- Been
- Before
- Best
- Big
- Black
- Blue
- Both
- Bottom
- Brown
- But
- Buy
- By
- Came
- Can
- Cold
- Come
- Could
- Did
- Do
- Does
- Don't
- Down
- Eat
- Every
- Fast
- Find
- First
- Five
- Fly
- For
- Found
- Fourth
- From
- Funny
- Gave
- Get
- Give
- Go
- Goes
- Going
- Good
- Grass
- Green
- Had

- Has
- Have
- He
- Help
- Her
- Him
- His
- How
- I
- In
- Into
- Is
- It
- Its
- Jump
- Just
- Knew
- Know
- Leaves
- Let
- Like
- Little
- Live
- Look
- Made
- Make
- Many
- May
- Me
- Must
- My
- No
- Not
- Now
- Of
- Off
- Old
- On
- Once
- One
- Open
- Or
- Our
- Out
- Over
- Play
- Please
- Pretty
- Pull
- Put
- Ran
- Read
- Red
- Ride
- Right
- Round
- Row
- Run
- Said
- Saw
- Say
- Second
- See

- She
- Sing
- Sit
- Sleep
- So
- Some
- Soon
- Stop
- Take
- Tell
- Thank
- That
- The
- Their
- Them
- Then
- There
- These
- They
- Think
- Third
- This
- Those
- Three
- To
- Too
- Top
- Tree
- Trunk
- Two
- Under
- Up
- Upon
- Us
- Use
- Very
- Walk
- Want
- Was
- Wash
- We
- Well
- Went
- Were
- What
- When
- Where
- Which
- White
- Who
- Why
- Will
- Wish
- With
- Work
- Would
- Write
- Yellow
- Yes
- You
- Your

Common Core State Standards

MATH:
K.G.A.1 Describe objects in the environment using names of shapes, and describe the relative position of these objects using terms such as *above, below, beside, in front of, behind,* and *next to.*

READING:
FOUNDATIONAL SKILLS, PHONICS, AND WORD RECOGNITION
RF.K.3, RF.1.3, RF.2.3 Know and apply grade-level phonics and word analysis skills in decoding words.
RF.K.3c Read common high-frequency words by sight.

FLUENCY
RF.K.4 Read emergent-reader texts with purpose and understanding.
RF.1.4, RF.2.4 Read with sufficient accuracy and fluency to support comprehension.

Apples Up on Top

Match Mine: Primary
Kagan Publishing • 1 (800) 933-2667 • www.KaganOnline.com

Apples Up on Top

Dolch Preprimer - 1

Cut out each game piece.

a	and	away	big
blue	can	come	down
find	for	funny	go
help	her	I	in
is	it	jump	little

Apples Up on Top

Dolch Preprimer - 2

Cut out each game piece.

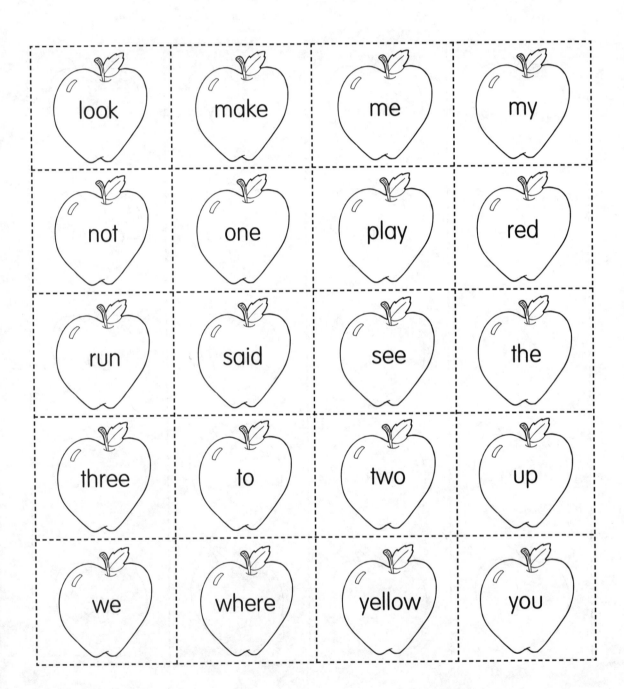

look	make	me	my
not	one	play	red
run	said	see	the
three	to	two	up
we	where	yellow	you

Match Mine: Primary
Kagan Publishing • 1 (800) 933-2667 • www.KaganOnline.com

Apples Up on Top

Dolch Primer - 1

Cut out each game piece.

all	am	are	at
ate	be	black	brown
but	came	did	do
eat	for	get	good
have	he	into	like

Apples Up on Top

Dolch Primer – 2 Cut out each game piece.

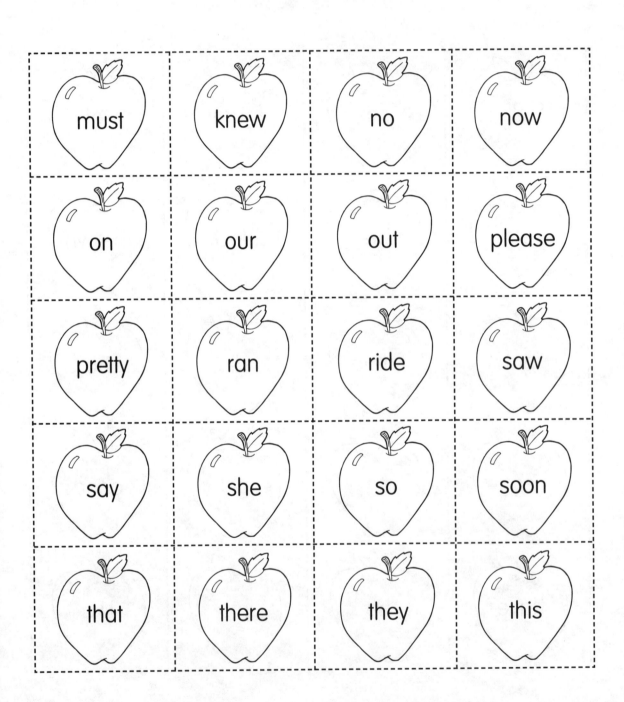

must	knew	no	now
on	our	out	please
pretty	ran	ride	saw
say	she	so	soon
that	there	they	this

Apples Up on Top

Dolch Primer – 3

Cut out each game piece.

too	under	want	was
well	went	what	white
who	will	with	yes

Apples Up on Top

Dolch Grade One – 1 Cut out each game piece.

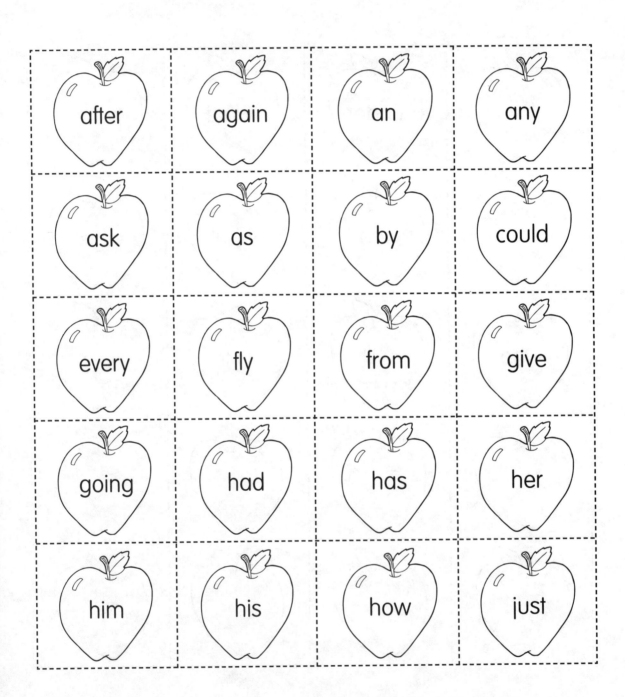

after	again	an	any
ask	as	by	could
every	fly	from	give
going	had	has	her
him	his	how	just

Match Mine: Primary
Kagan Publishing • 1 (800) 933-2667 • www.KaganOnline.com

Apples Up on Top

Dolch Grade One – 2
Cut out each game piece.

know	let	live	may
of	old	once	open
over	put	round	some
stop	take	thank	them
then	think	walk	were

Apples Up on Top

Dolch Grade Two – 1

Cut out each game piece.

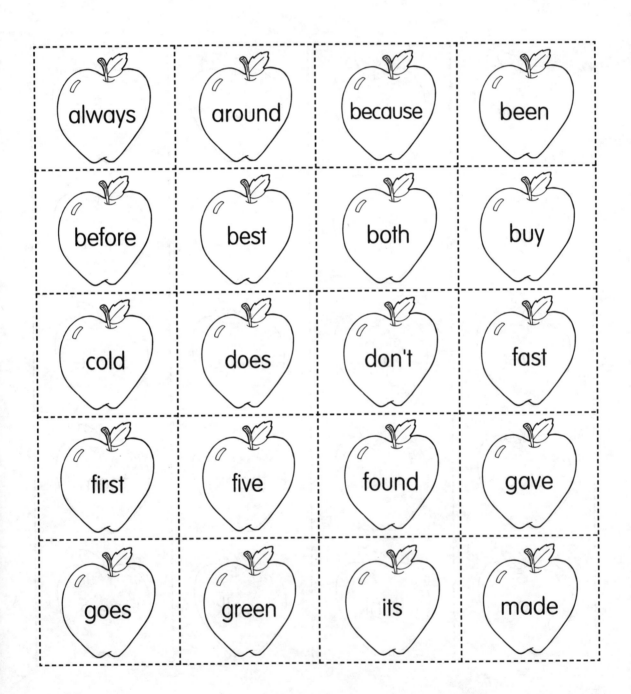

always	around	because	been
before	best	both	buy
cold	does	don't	fast
first	five	found	gave
goes	green	its	made

Match Mine: Primary
Kagan Publishing • 1 (800) 933-2667 • www.KaganOnline.com

Apples Up on Top

Dolch Grade Two - 2

Cut out each game piece.

many	off	or	pull
read	right	sing	sit
sleep	their	tell	these
those	upon	us	use
very	wash	when	which

Apples Up on Top

Dolch Grade Two – 3   Cut out each game piece.

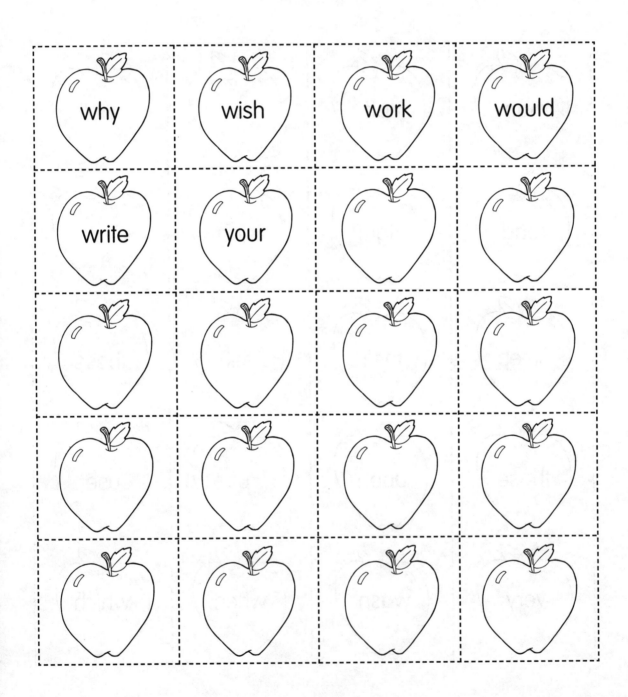

Match Mine: Primary
Kagan Publishing • 1 (800) 933-2667 • www.KaganOnline.com

Astro Talk

Partner A sends one direction at a time, telling Partner B where to place the shapes on the Astro Talk game board. Partner B cooperates with Partner A to make a match.

Game Board

Game Pieces

Vocabulary

- Above
- Astronaut
- Below
- Beside
- Circle
- Hexagon
- Left
- Next to
- On top of
- Oval
- Rectangle
- Rhombus
- Right
- Shape
- Square
- Triangle

Common Core State Standards

MATH:
K.G.A.1 Describe objects in the environment using names of shapes, and describe the relative position of these objects using terms such as *above, below, beside, in front of, behind,* and *next to.*

SPEAKING & LISTENING:
COMPREHENSION AND COLLABORATION
SL.K.1a, SL.1.1a, SL.2.1a Follow agreed-upon rules for discussions.
SL.K.3, SL.1.3, SL.2.3 Ask and answer questions in order to seek help, get information, or clarify something that is not understood.

PRESENTATION OF KNOWLEDGE AND IDEAS
SL.K.6 Speak audibly and express thoughts, feelings, and ideas clearly.
SL.1.6, SL.2.6 Produce complete sentences when appropriate to task and situation.

Astro Talk

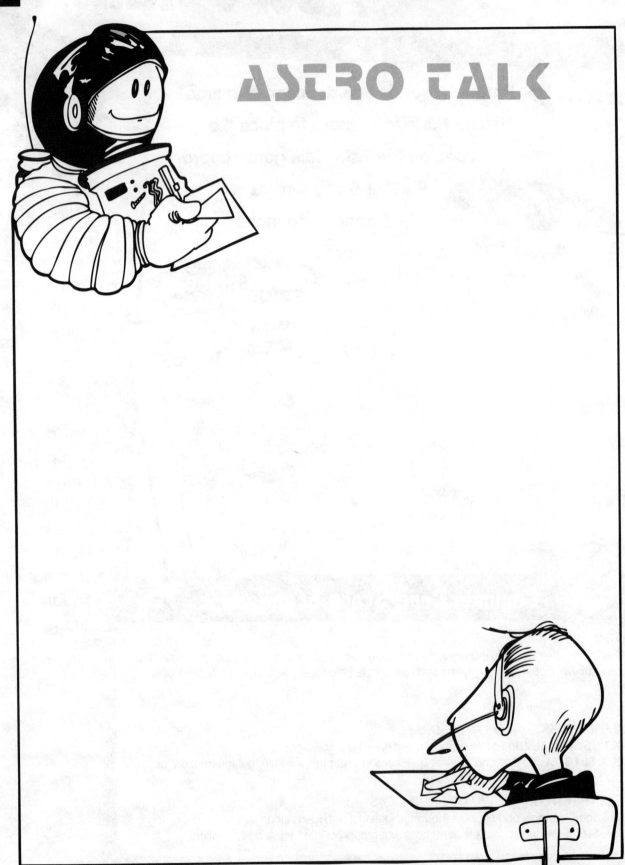

Astro Talk

Game Pieces – Partner A   Cut out each shape.

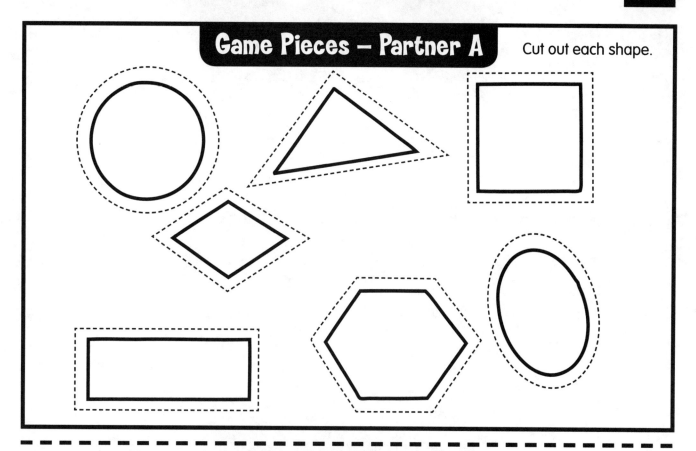

Game Pieces – Partner B   Cut out each shape.

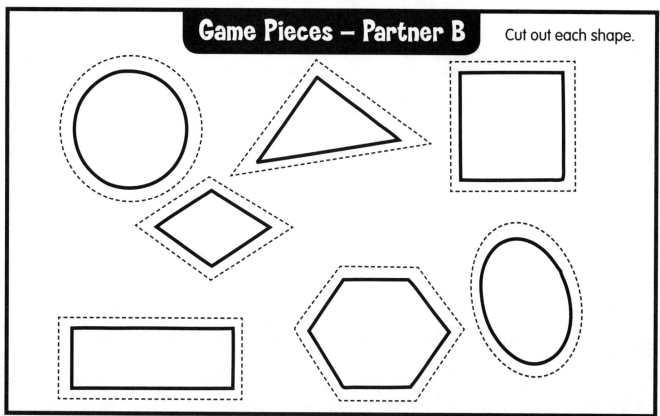

BzZzZ

Partner A reads the beginning sound, blend, or digraph letter name game piece and tells Partner B to find a corresponding picture with the same beginning sound, blend, or digraph and place it on the beehive on the BzZzZ game board. Partner B cooperates with Partner A to make a match.

Game Board

BzZzZ

Game 3

Game Pieces

BzZzZ

Beginning Sound Letters – 1   Game 3

Cut out each game piece.

Differentiation

Differentiation is built into the game piece selection. You can have students match picture to picture for beginning sounds, blends or digraphs, with Sender and Receiver having different pictures representing the same sound. You can also have students match picture to letter/sound association of picture to letters that represent beginning blends or digraphs. You can even have students simply match letter/sound associations for letters representing blends and digraphs.

Common Core State Standards

MATH:
K.G.A.1 Describe objects in the environment using names of shapes, and describe the relative position of these objects using terms such as *above, below, beside, in front of, behind*, and *next to*.

READING:
FOUNDATIONAL SKILLS, PHONOLOGICAL AWARENESS
RF.K.2d Isolate and pronounce initial, medial vowel, and final sounds (phonemes) in three-phoneme words.
RF.1.2c Isolate and pronounce initial, media, vowel and final sounds (phonemes) in spoken single syllable words.

PHONICS AND WORD RECOGNITION
RF.K.3a Demonstrate basic knowledge of one-to-one letter-sound correspondences by producing the primary sound or many of the most frequent sounds for each consonant.

Vocabulary

- Apple
- Bath
- Bee
- Beehive
- Blender
- Blimp
- Block
- Blow
- Brain
- Bread
- Bricks
- Bridge
- Broom
- Brush
- Bus
- Bush
- Carrot
- Catch
- Chain
- Chair
- Cheese
- Cherries
- Clap
- Climb
- Clock
- Cloud
- Crab
- Crayon
- Crown
- Cry
- Die
- Dress
- Drill
- Drip
- Drum
- Eggs
- Feather
- Fish
- Flag
- Flashlight
- Flower
- Fly
- Freeze
- Fries
- Frog
- Fruit
- Glasses
- Globe
- Gloves
- Glue
- Grapes
- Grass
- Grasshopper
- Grave
- Horse
- Igloo
- Jam
- Judge
- Key
- Knee
- Knife
- Knot
- Lion
- Moon
- Nest
- Octopus
- Pharoah
- Phone
- Photo
- Photographer
- Plane
- Plate
- Playground
- Plug
- Popcorn
- Pray
- Present
- Pretzel
- Princess
- Queen
- Question
- Quilt
- Ring
- Rocks
- Shark
- Sheep
- Shell
- Ship
- Sign
- Sing
- Skateboard
- Skeleton
- Ski
- Skunk
- Sleep
- Sled
- Slice
- Slide
- Smell
- Smile
- Smoke
- Smear
- Snail
- Snake
- Snore
- Snowman
- Socks
- Spider
- Spill
- Spoon
- Spy
- Stamp
- Star
- Stork
- Stove
- Sweater
- Sweep
- Swim
- Swing
- Thermometer
- Thorn
- Thread
- Thumb
- Tooth
- Trashcan
- Tractor
- Tree
- Triangle
- Turtle
- Twenty
- Twig
- Twins
- Twist
- Umbrella
- Violin
- Walrus
- Watch
- Whale
- Wheel
- Wheelchair
- Whistle
- Wing
- Writing
- X-ray
- Yak
- Zipper

BzZzZ

Match Mine: Primary
Kagan Publishing • 1 (800) 933-2667 • www.KaganOnline.com

BzZzZ

Game 3

Beginning Sound Letters - 1

Cut out each game piece.

Aa	Bb	Cc	Dd
Ee	Ff	Gg	Hh
Ii	Jj	Kk	Ll
Mm	Nn	Oo	Pp
Qq	Rr	Ss	Tt
Uu	Vv	Ww	Xx
Yy	Zz		

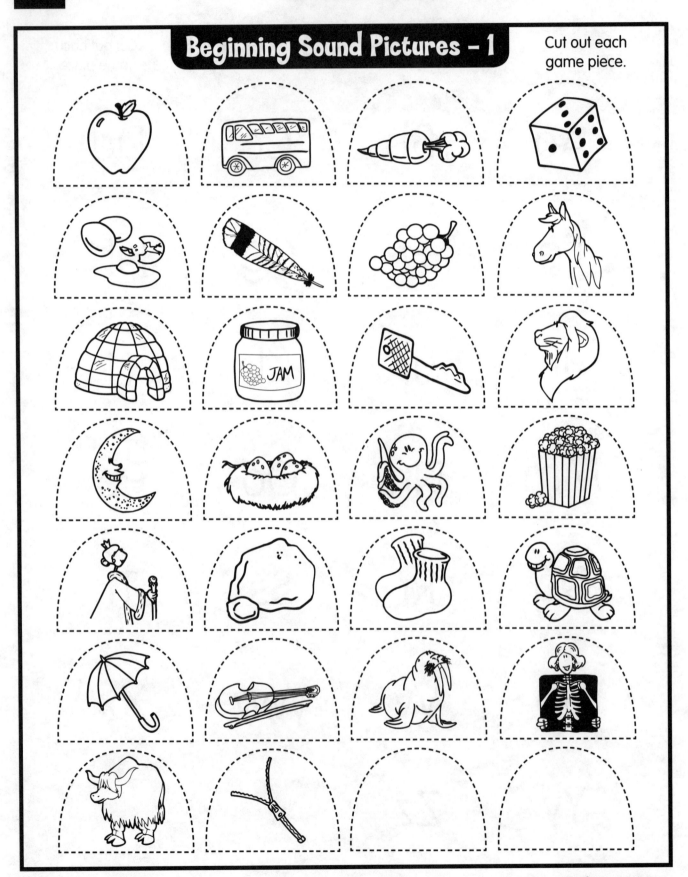

BzZzZ

Beginning Sound Pictures – 1

Cut out each
game piece.

Match Mine: Primary

Kagan Publishing • 1 (800) 933-2667 • www.KaganOnline.com

Digraph Letters – 1

Cut out each game piece.

ch- th- sh- ph-

kn- wh- wr- qu-

-gn -sh -th -dge

-tch -ng

BzZzZ

Digraph Pictures – 1

Cut out each game piece.

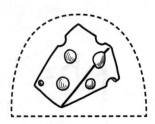   

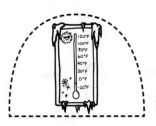   

   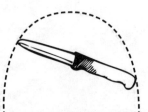

Match Mine: Primary
Kagan Publishing • 1 (800) 933-2667 • www.KaganOnline.com

BzZzZ

Digraph Pictures - 2
Cut out each game piece.

   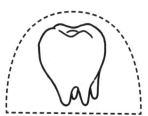

BzZzZ

bl

fl

gl

br

cl

sl

fr

sn

cr

st

sp

tr

dr

pl

sw

gr

sm

tw

pr

sk

Match Mine: Primary
Kagan Publishing • 1 (800) 933-2667 • www.KaganOnline.com

BzZzZ

Blend Pictures – 1

Cut out each game piece.

   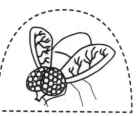

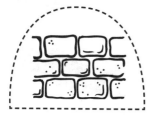   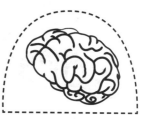

BzZzZ

Blend Pictures - 2

Cut out each game piece.

Match Mine: Primary
Kagan Publishing • 1 (800) 933-2667 • www.KaganOnline.com

BzZzZ

Blend Pictures - 3

Cut out each game piece.

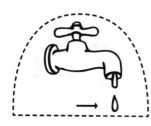   

BZZzZ

Blend Pictures – 4

Cut out each game piece.

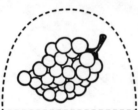

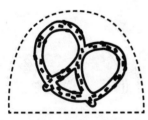

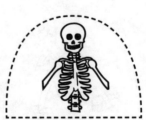

Match Mine: Primary
Kagan Publishing • 1 (800) 933-2667 • www.KaganOnline.com

BzZzZ

Game Pieces – Blank Template

Cut out each
game piece.

Community Helpers

Partner A chooses a Community Helpers game piece, then asks Partner B to find the same game piece and place it on a specific place on the game board. Partner B cooperates with Partner A to make a match.

Game Board

Game Pieces

Vocabulary

- Above
- Baker
- Behind
- Below
- Beside
- Carpenter
- Chef
- Dentist
- Doctor
- Firewoman
- Hairstylist
- In front of
- Mailman
- Next to
- Nurse
- Painter
- Pilot
- Policeman
- Seamstress
- Travel agent
- Veterinarian
- Waitress

Common Core State Standards

MATH:
K.G.A.1 Describe objects in the environment using names of shapes, and describe the relative position of these objects using terms such as *above, below, beside, in front of, behind,* and *next to.*

SPEAKING & LISTENING:
COMPREHENSION AND COLLABORATION
SL.K.1a, SL.1.1a, SL.2.1a Follow agreed-upon rules for discussions.
SL.K.3, SL.1.3, SL.2.3 Ask and answer questions in order to seek help, get information, or clarify something that is not understood.

PRESENTATION OF KNOWLEDGE AND IDEAS
SL.K.6 Speak audibly and express thoughts, feelings, and ideas clearly.
SL.1.6, SL.2.6 Produce complete sentences when appropriate to task and situation.

Community Helpers

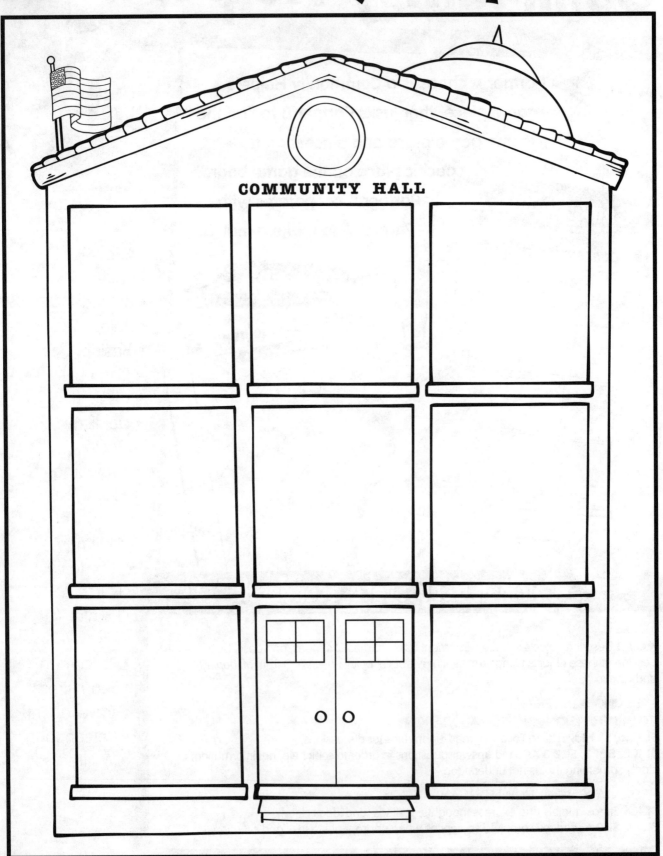

COMMUNITY HALL

Match Mine: Primary
Kagan Publishing • 1 (800) 933-2667 • www.KaganOnline.com

Community Helpers

Game Pieces – Partner A

Cut out each
game piece.

Community Helpers

Game Pieces – Partner B

Cut out each game piece.

Match Mine: Primary
Kagan Publishing • 1 (800) 933-2667 • www.KaganOnline.com

Country Hoedown

Partner A reads the picture game piece and tells Partner B to find the corresponding rhyming picture and place it on a specific place on the Country Hoedown game board. Partner B cooperates with Partner A to make a match.

Game Board

Country Hoedown

Game Pieces

Country Hoedown

Game Pieces – Partner A

Cut out each rhyming game piece.

Game Pieces – Partner B

Cut out each rhyming game piece.

Rhyming Word Pairs

- Car–Star
- Sun–Bun
- Bell–Shell
- Sock–Rock
- Goat–Coat
- Bee–Tree
- Rice–Ice
- Bed–Sled
- Sheep–Jeep

Vocabulary

- Bed
- Bee
- Bell
- Bun
- Car
- Coat
- Goat
- Hay bale
- Horse
- Ice
- Jeep
- Pig
- Rice
- Rock
- Sheep
- Shell
- Sled
- Sock
- Star
- Sun
- Tree

Common Core State Standards

MATH:
K.G.A.1 Describe objects in the environment using names of shapes, and describe the relative position of these objects using terms such as *above, below, beside, in front of, behind*, and *next to*.

READING:
FOUNDATIONAL SKILLS, PHONOLOGICAL AWARENESS
RF.K.2a Recognize and produce rhyming words.

Country Hoedown

Match Mine: Primary

Kagan Publishing • 1 (800) 933-2667 • www.KaganOnline.com

Country Hoedown

Game Pieces – Partner A

Cut out each rhyming game piece.

Game Pieces – Partner B

Cut out each rhyming game piece.

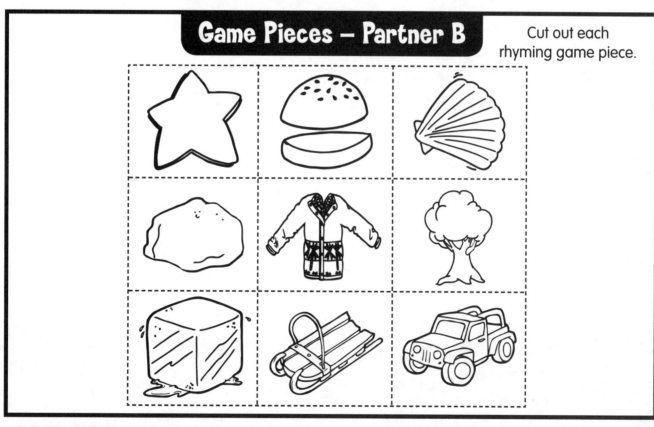

Decorate It!

Partner A reads the word family ending game piece and tells Partner B to find a corresponding word family picture and place it on the Decorate It! game board. Partner B cooperates with Partner A to make a match.

Vocabulary

• Bag	• Lid
• Ball	• Lip
• Bean	• Log
• Bear	• Lunch
• Bed	• Mad
• Book	• Moth
• Bug	• Mud
• Bump	• Nurse
• Cake	• Pig
• Can	• Pin
• Candles	• Plane
• Card	• Pot
• Cat	• Rain
• Clock	• Ring
• Clown	• Run
• Coin	• Seed
• Cow	• Send
• Cut	• Sheep
• Drum	• Sick
• Duck	• Skate
• Fish	• Snail
• Game	• Star
• Gem	• Store
• Grade	• Top
• Grape	• Toy
• Hand	• Trash
• Jet	• Tub
• Lake	• Web
• Leg	• Well

Game Board

Decorate It!

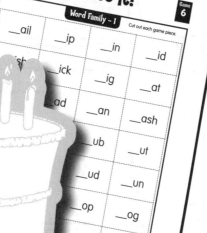

Game Pieces

Decorate It!

Word Family – 1   Cut out each game piece.

__ail	__ip	__in	__id
__ish	__ick	__ig	__at
__ad	__an	__ash	
	__ub	__ut	
	__ud	__un	
	__op	__og	
	__ore	__ook	

Common Core State Standards

MATH:
K.G.A.1 Describe objects in the environment using names of shapes, and describe the relative position of these objects using terms such as *above, below, beside, in front of, behind,* and *next to.*

READING:
FOUNDATIONAL SKILLS, PHONOLOGICAL AWARENESS
RF.K.2c Blend and segment onsets and rimes of single-syllable spoken words.
RF.1.3a Know the spelling-sound correspondences for common consonant digraphs.

Decorate It!

Match Mine: Primary

Kagan Publishing • 1 (800) 933-2667 • www.KaganOnline.com

Decorate It!

Word Family – 1   Cut out each game piece.

__ail	__ip	__in	__id
__ish	__ick	__ig	__at
__ag	__ad	__an	__ash
__and	__all	__ub	__ut
__ug	__um	__ud	__un
__uck	__unch	__op	__og
__ock	__ot	__ore	__ook

Decorate It!

Cut out each
game piece.

Match Mine: Primary
Kagan Publishing • 1 (800) 933-2667 • www.KaganOnline.com

Decorate It!

Word Family - 2

Cut out each game piece.

__oth	__et	__em	__eg
__ed	__eb	__end	__urse
__ell	__ar	__ard	__ear
__ean	__ing	__ow	__own
__ump	__ame	__ate	__ain
__ane	__ape	__ake	__ade
__eed	__eep	__oy	__oin

Decorate It!

Pictures for Word Family - 2

Cut out each game piece.

Match Mine: Primary
Kagan Publishing • 1 (800) 933-2667 • www.KaganOnline.com

Decorate It!

Game Pieces – Blank Template

Cut out each game piece.

Farm Fun

Partner A sends one direction at a time, telling Partner B where to place the farm game pieces on the Farm Fun game board. Partner B cooperates with Partner A to make a match.

Game Board

Game Pieces

Vocabulary

- Above
- Basket
- Behind
- Below
- Cat
- Chick
- Cow
- Dog
- Hay bale
- Frog
- In front of
- In back of
- On top of
- Rabbit
- Tractor
- Worm

Common Core State Standards

MATH:
K.G.A.1 Describe objects in the environment using names of shapes, and describe the relative position of these objects using terms such as *above, below, beside, in front of, behind,* and *next to.*

SPEAKING & LISTENING:
COMPREHENSION AND COLLABORATION
SL.K.1a, SL.1.1a, SL.2.1a Follow agreed-upon rules for discussions.
SL.K.3, SL.1.3, SL.2.3 Ask and answer questions in order to seek help, get information, or clarify something that is not understood.

PRESENTATION OF KNOWLEDGE AND IDEAS
SL.K.6 Speak audibly and express thoughts, feelings, and ideas clearly.
SL.1.6, SL.2.6 Produce complete sentences when appropriate to task and situation.

Farm Fun

Match Mine: Primary

Farm Fun

Partner A

Cut out each game piece.

Partner B

Cut out each game piece.

Go Fish

Partner A chooses an ending sound game piece, then asks Partner B to choose a picture game piece with the corresponding ending sound and place it on the Go Fish game board. Partner B cooperates with Partner A to make a match.

Vocabulary

- Bed
- Boy
- Cat
- Catch
- Corn
- Crab
- First
- Fish
- Fishing pole
- Five
- Leaf
- Mouse
- Seal
- Second
- Splash
- Tag
- Third
- Top
- Truck
- Worm

Game Board

Game Pieces

Common Core State Standards

MATH:
K.G.A.1 Describe objects in the environment using names of shapes, and describe the relative position of these objects using terms such as *above, below, beside, in front of, behind,* and *next to*.

READING:
FOUNDATIONAL SKILLS, PHONOLOGICAL AWARENESS
RF.K.2d Isolate and pronounce initial, medial vowel, and final sounds (phonemes) in three-phoneme words.
RF.1.2c Isolate and pronounce initial, medial vowel, and final sounds (phonemes) in spoken single syllable words.

Go Fish

Match Mine: Primary
Kagan Publishing • 1 (800) 933-2667 • www.KaganOnline.com

Go Fish

Game Pieces – Partner A

Cut out each game piece.

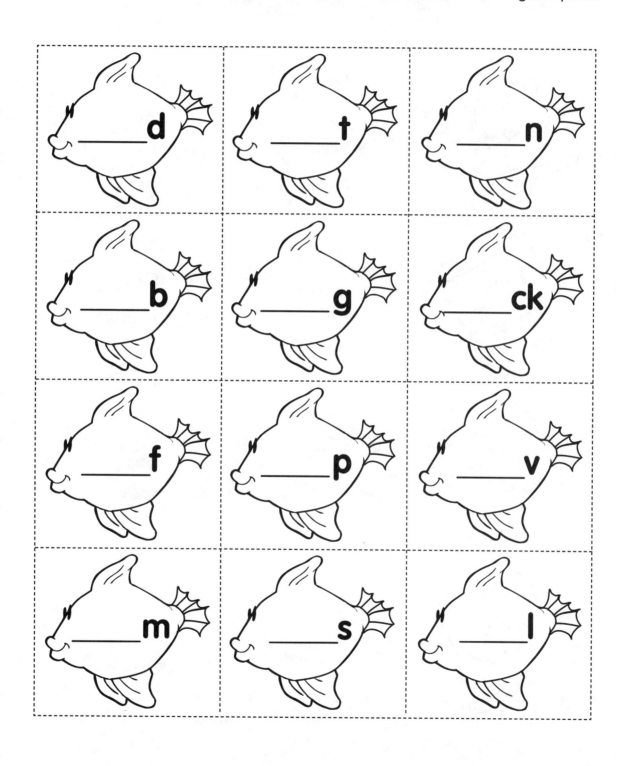

Go Fish

Game Pieces – Partner B

Cut out each game piece.

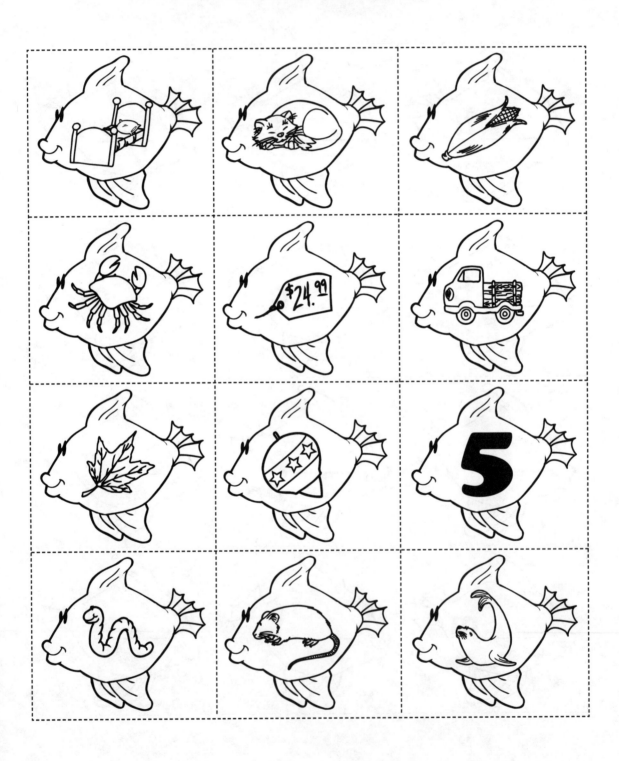

Match Mine: Primary

Kagan Publishing • 1 (800) 933-2667 • www.KaganOnline.com

Gumball Wizard

Partner A chooses a cents or a coins game piece, then asks Partner B to choose a game piece with the corresponding cents or coins and place it on a specific place on the Gumball Wizard game board. Partner B cooperates with Partner A to make a match.

Game Board

Gumball Wizard

Game Pieces

Gumball Wizard
Cents Game Pieces (1¢–20¢) Cut out each gumball

1¢ 3¢ 4¢

Differentiation

Differentiation is built into the game piece selection. You can have students match coin value (cents) to coins representing the same value for example, the Sender has 14¢ and the Receiver has a dime and four pennies. You can also have students match different coins that represent the same value for example, Sender has a dime and Receiver has two nickels. Another variation is Sender has the head side of the coins and Receiver has the tail side of the coins, or heads and tails coins are mixed.

Vocabulary

- Bottom
- Cents (¢)
- Coin
- Coin counting
- Coin identification
- Dime
- First
- Fourth
- Gumball
- Gumball machine
- Middle
- Nickel
- Penny
- Quarter
- Row
- Second
- Third
- Top
- Value

Common Core State Standards

MATH:
K.G.A.1 Describe objects in the environment using names of shapes, and describe the relative position of these objects using terms such as *above, below, beside, in front of, behind,* and *next to.*

MEASUREMENT AND DATA
2.MD.C.8 Solve word problems involving dollar bills, quarters, dimes, nickels, and pennies, using $ and ¢ symbols appropriately.

Gumball Wizard

Match Mine: Primary
Kagan Publishing • 1 (800) 933-2667 • www.KaganOnline.com

Gumball Wizard

Cents Game Pieces (1¢–20¢)

Cut out each gumball.

1¢   3¢   4¢

6¢   7¢   10¢

12¢   13¢   15¢

16¢   19¢   20¢

Gumball Wizard

Cents Game Pieces (37¢–50¢)

Cut out each gumball.

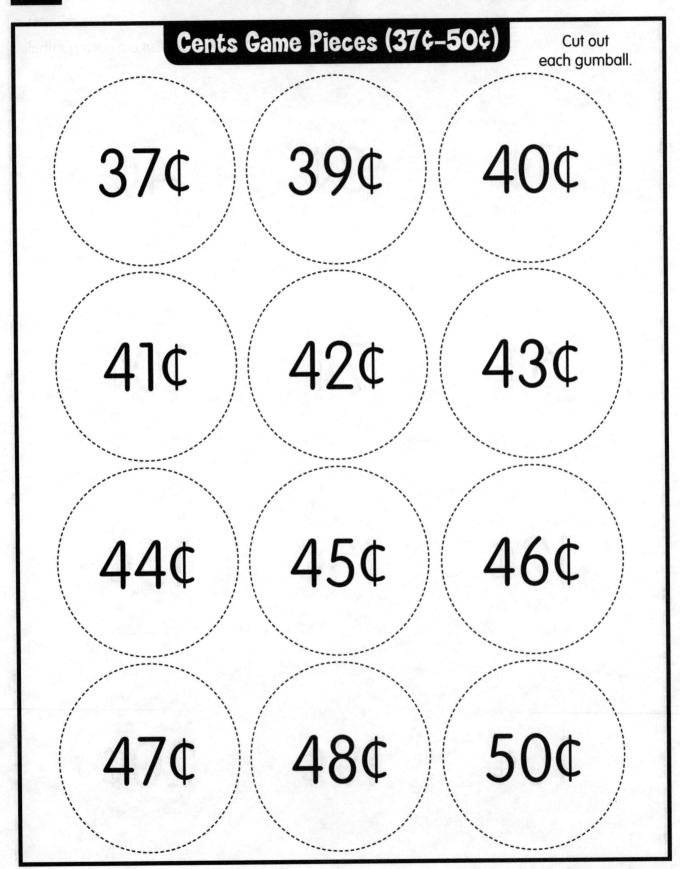

37¢ 39¢ 40¢

41¢ 42¢ 43¢

44¢ 45¢ 46¢

47¢ 48¢ 50¢

Match Mine: Primary

Kagan Publishing • 1 (800) 933-2667 • www.KaganOnline.com

Gumball Wizard

Coin Heads/Tails Game Pieces (1¢–20¢)

Cut out each gumball.

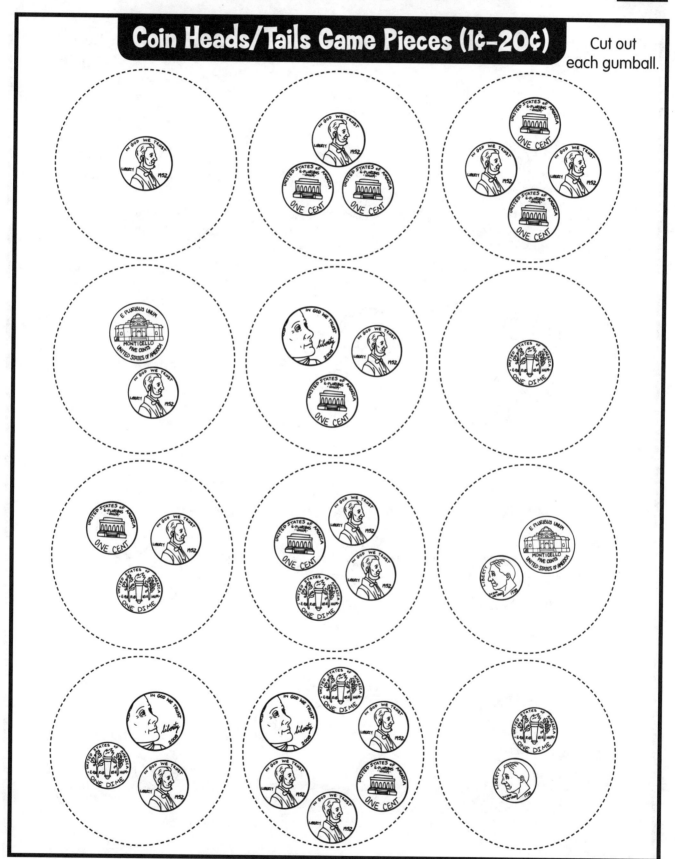

Gumball Wizard

Coin Heads Game Pieces (1¢–20¢)

Cut out
each gumball.

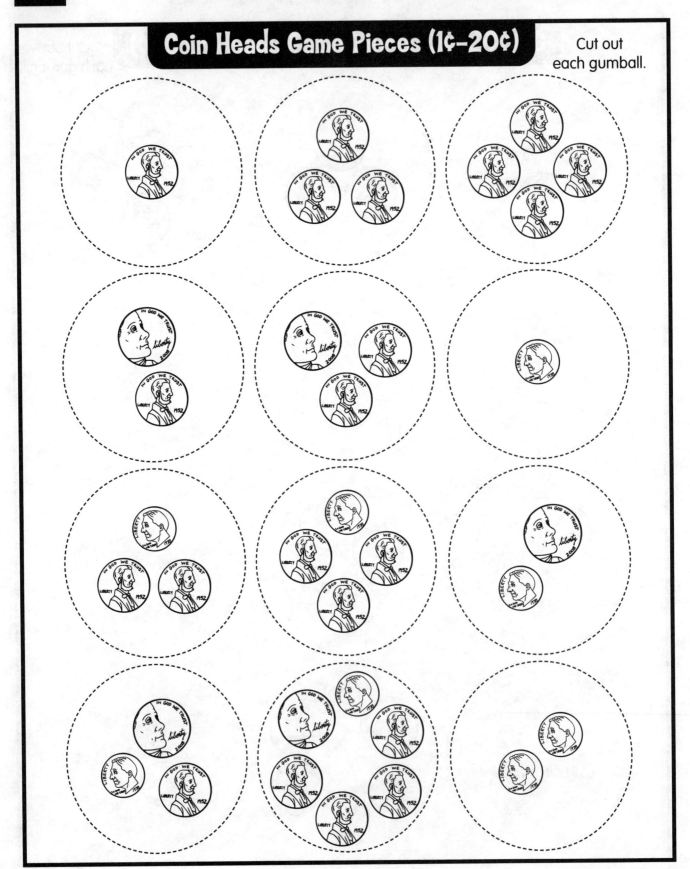

Match Mine: Primary
Kagan Publishing • 1 (800) 933-2667 • www.KaganOnline.com

Gumball Wizard

Coin Tails Game Pieces (1¢–20¢)

Cut out each gumball.

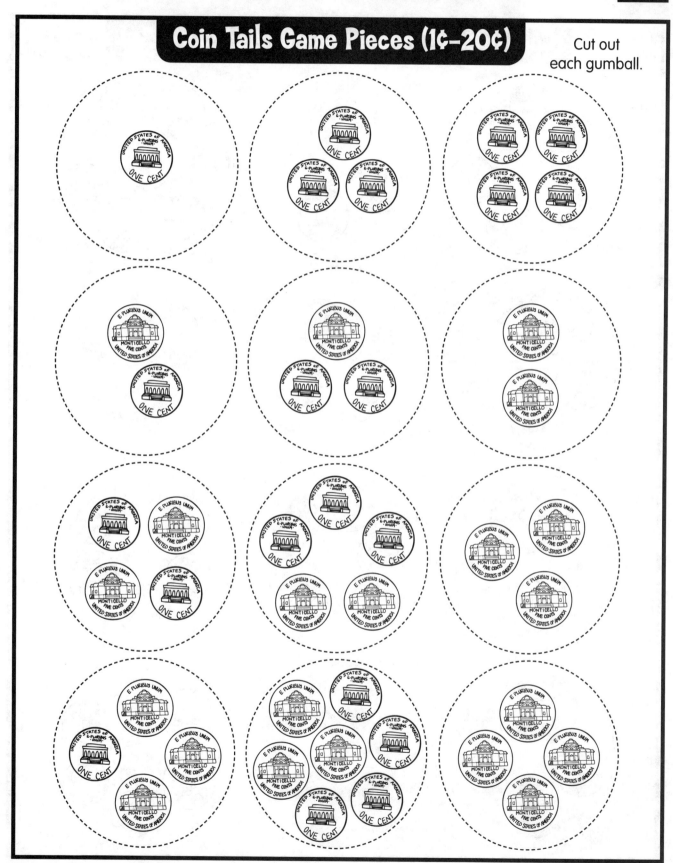

Gumball Wizard

Coin Heads/Tails Game Pieces (37¢–43¢)

Cut out
each gumball.

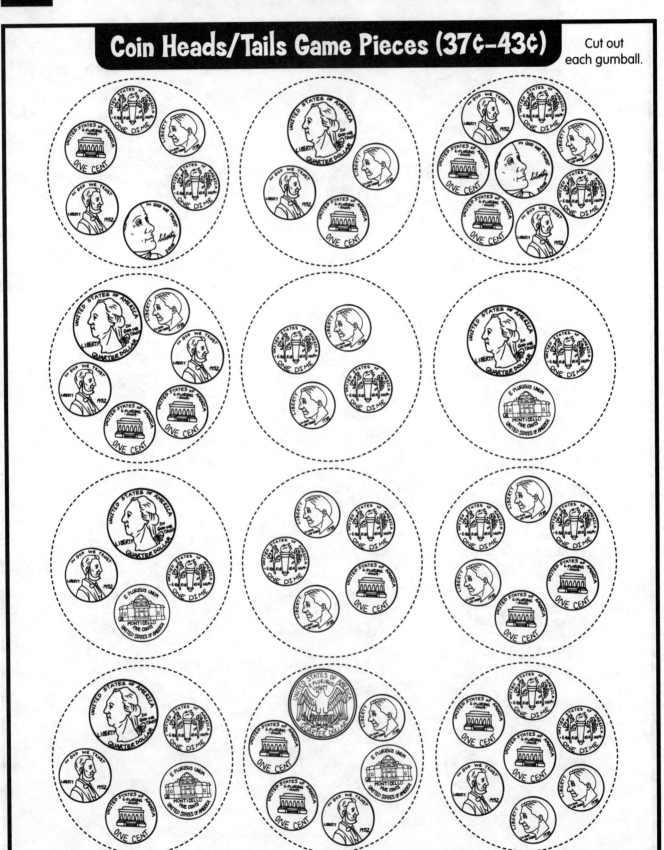

Gumball Wizard

Coin Heads/Tails Game Pieces (44¢–50¢)

Cut out each gumball.

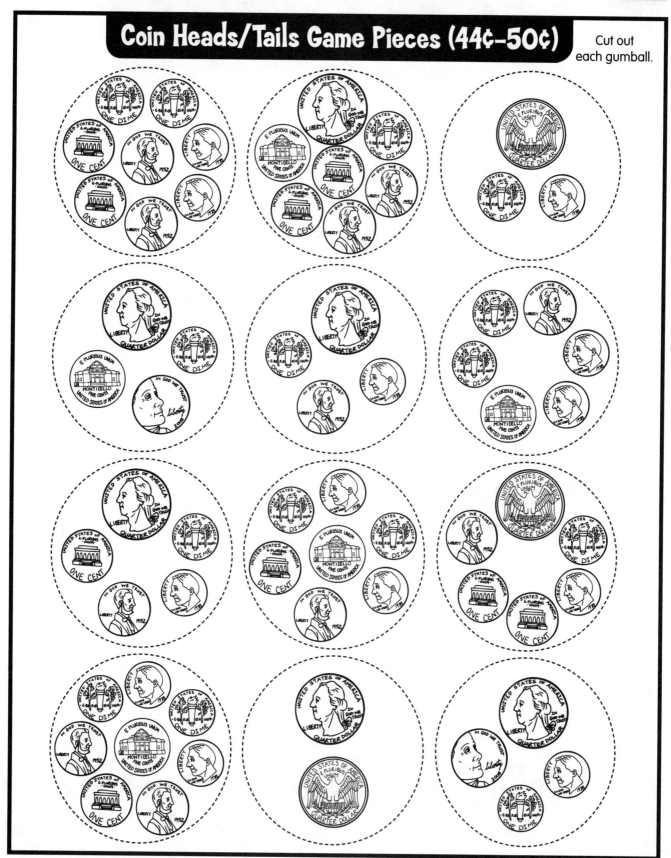

Jammin' Out the Number Rock!

Partner A chooses a game piece, then asks Partner B to choose a game piece to compose or decompose the addition sentence and place it on the Jammin' Out game board. Partner B cooperates with Partner A to make a match.

Game Board

Jammin' Out the Number Rock!

Game Pieces

Jammin' Out the Number Rock!

Number Game Pieces – 1

Cut out each game piece.

8	6	10
6	2	1
4	10	9
0	8	4
3	5	7
1	1	1
2	3	3
1	3	6
	2	3

Vocabulary

- Addition
- Bottom
- Compose
- Decompose
- Dots
- First
- Fourth
- Jukebox
- Music
- Musical notes
- Numbers
- Row
- Second
- Third
- Top

Differentiation

Depending on your students' level of number concepts, you can choose composing or decomposing numbers with either numbers or dots. You can also start with Partner A having the dots and Partner B having the dots or the numeral to represent the number of dots.

Common Core State Standards

MATH:
OPERATIONS AND ALGEBRAIC THINKING, ADD AND SUBTRACT WITHIN 20
K.G.A.1 Describe objects in the environment using names of shapes, and describe the relative position of these objects using terms such as *above, below, beside, in front of, behind,* and *next to.*
K.OA.A.3 Decompose numbers less than or equal to 10 into pairs in more than one way.
K.OA.A.5 Fluently add and subtract within 5.
1.OA.C.5 Relate counting to addition and subtraction.
1.OA.C.6 Add and subtract within 20, demonstrating fluency for addition and subtraction within 10.
2.OA.B.2 Fluently add and subtract within 20 using mental strategies. By end of Grade 2, know from memory all sums of two 1-digit numbers.

Jammin' Out the Number Rock!

Match Mine: Primary
Kagan Publishing • 1 (800) 933-2667 • www.KaganOnline.com

Jammin' Out the Number Rock!

Number Game Pieces – 1

Cut out each game piece.

8		6		10	
	6	2			1

4		10		9	
0			8	4	

3		5		7	
	1	1			3

2		3		6	
1			2	3	

7		5		10	
	5	4			5

8		9		6	
3			3	5	

7		10		9	
0			4	1	

3		8		10	
	0	4			9

Jammin' Out the Number Rock!

Number Game Pieces – 2

Cut out each game piece.

2	**4**	**9**
4	**2**	**5**
2	**4**	**4**
1	**1**	**3**
2	**1**	**5**
5	**6**	**1**
7	**6**	**8**
3	**4**	**1**

Match Mine: Primary
Kagan Publishing • 1 (800) 933-2667 • www.KaganOnline.com

Jammin' Out the Number Rock!

Dot Game Pieces - 1

Cut out each game piece.

Jammin' Out the Number Rock!

Dot Game Pieces – 2

Cut out each game piece.

Match Mine: Primary
Kagan Publishing • 1 (800) 933-2667 • www.KaganOnline.com

Just Chilling

Partner A chooses a penguin game piece with two words, then asks Partner B to find the game piece with the corresponding contraction and place it on the Just Chilling game board. Partner B cooperates with Partner A to make a match.

Game Board

Just Chilling

Game Pieces

Just Chilling
Word Game Pieces - 1
Cut out each game piece.

I will
I am
I would

Vocabulary

- Bottom
- Contractions
- First
- Iceberg
- Middle
- Penguin
- Second
- Third
- Top

Contractions

- Are not–Aren't
- Can not–Can't
- Could have–Could've
- Could not–Couldn't
- Did not–Didn't
- Do not–Don't
- Had not–Hadn't
- Has not–Hasn't
- He had–He'd
- He has–He's
- He is–He's
- He will–He'll
- He would–He'd
- Here is–Here's

- I am–I'm
- I had–I'd
- I have–I've
- I will–I'll
- I would–I'd
- Is not–Isn't
- She had–She'd
- She has–She's
- She is–She's
- She will–She'll
- She would–She'd
- Should have–Should've
- Should not–Shouldn't
- That is–That's

- They will–They'll
- They had–They'd
- They would–They'd
- There is–There's
- They are–They're
- They have–They've
- Was not–Wasn't
- We are–We're
- We had–We'd
- We have–We've
- We will–We'll
- We would–We'd
- Were not–Weren't
- What is–what's

- Where has–Where's
- Who has–Who's
- Who is–Who's
- Who will–Who'll
- Who would–who'd
- Would have–Would've
- Would not–Wouldn't
- You are–You're
- You had–You'd
- You have–You've
- You will–You'll
- You would–You'd

Common Core State Standards

MATH:

K.G.A.1 Describe objects in the environment using names of shapes, and describe the relative position of these objects using terms such as *above, below, beside, in front of, behind,* and *next to.*

LANGUAGE:

CONVENTIONS OF STANDARD ENGLISH

L.2.2c Use an apostrophe to form contractions and frequently occurring possessives.

Just Chilling

Match Mine: Primary
Kagan Publishing • 1 (800) 933-2667 • www.KaganOnline.com

Just Chilling

Word Game Pieces – 1

Cut out each game piece.

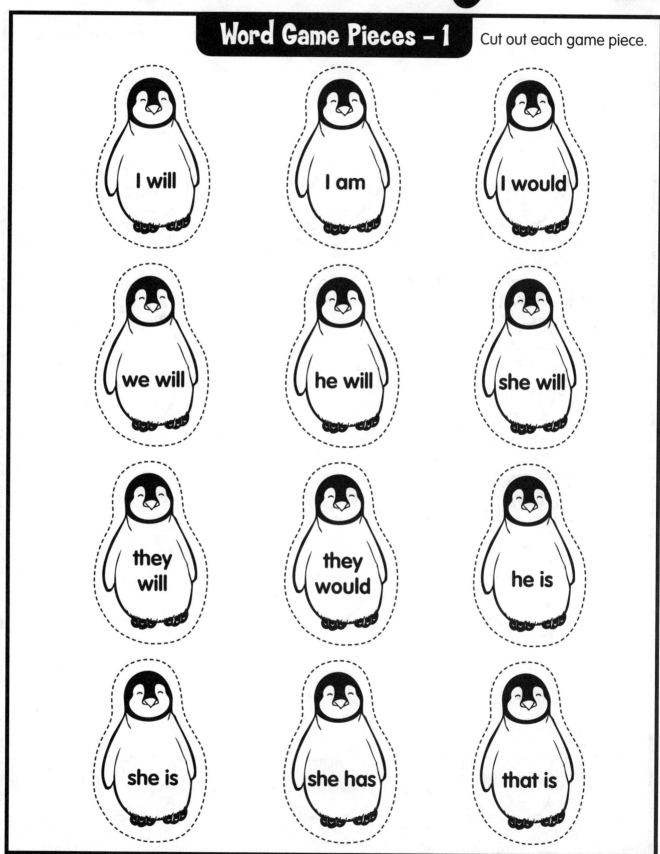

I will

I am

I would

we will

he will

she will

they will

they would

he is

she is

she has

that is

Just Chilling

Word Game Pieces – 2

Cut out each game piece.

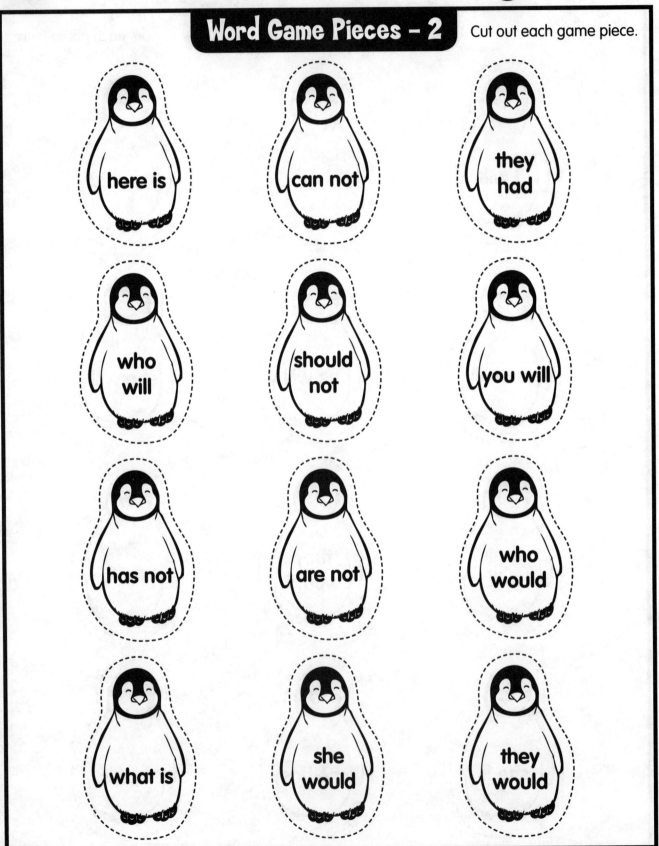

here is

can not

they had

who will

should not

you will

has not

are not

who would

what is

she would

they would

Match Mine: Primary
Kagan Publishing • 1 (800) 933-2667 • www.KaganOnline.com

Just Chilling

Word Game Pieces - 3
Cut out each game piece.

there is

who is

we had

we are

I had

had not

he has

they are

is not

where has

he had

you had

Just Chilling

Word Game Pieces – 4   Cut out each game piece.

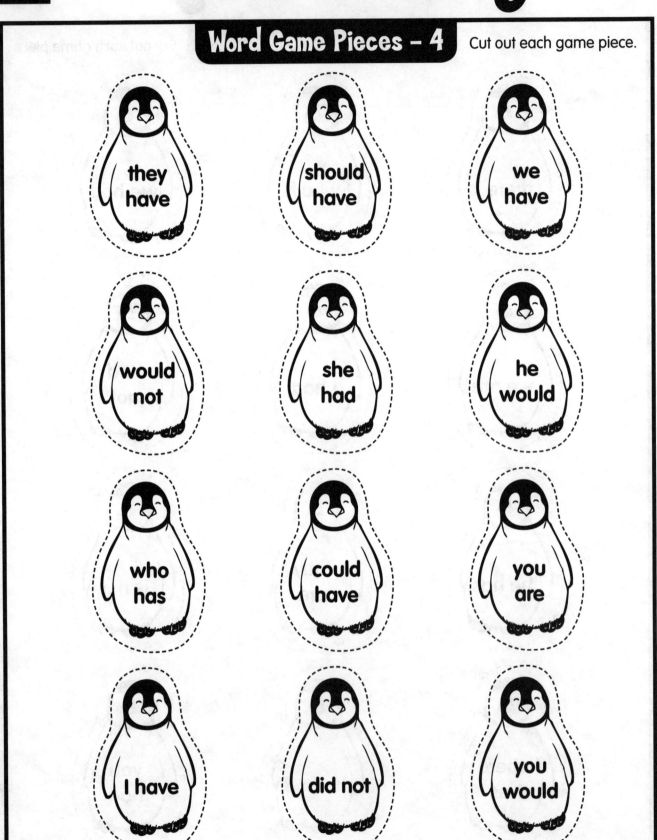

they have

should have

we have

would not

she had

he would

who has

could have

you are

I have

did not

you would

Match Mine: Primary
Kagan Publishing • 1 (800) 933-2667 • www.KaganOnline.com

Just Chilling

Game 11

Word Game Pieces – 5

Cut out each game piece.

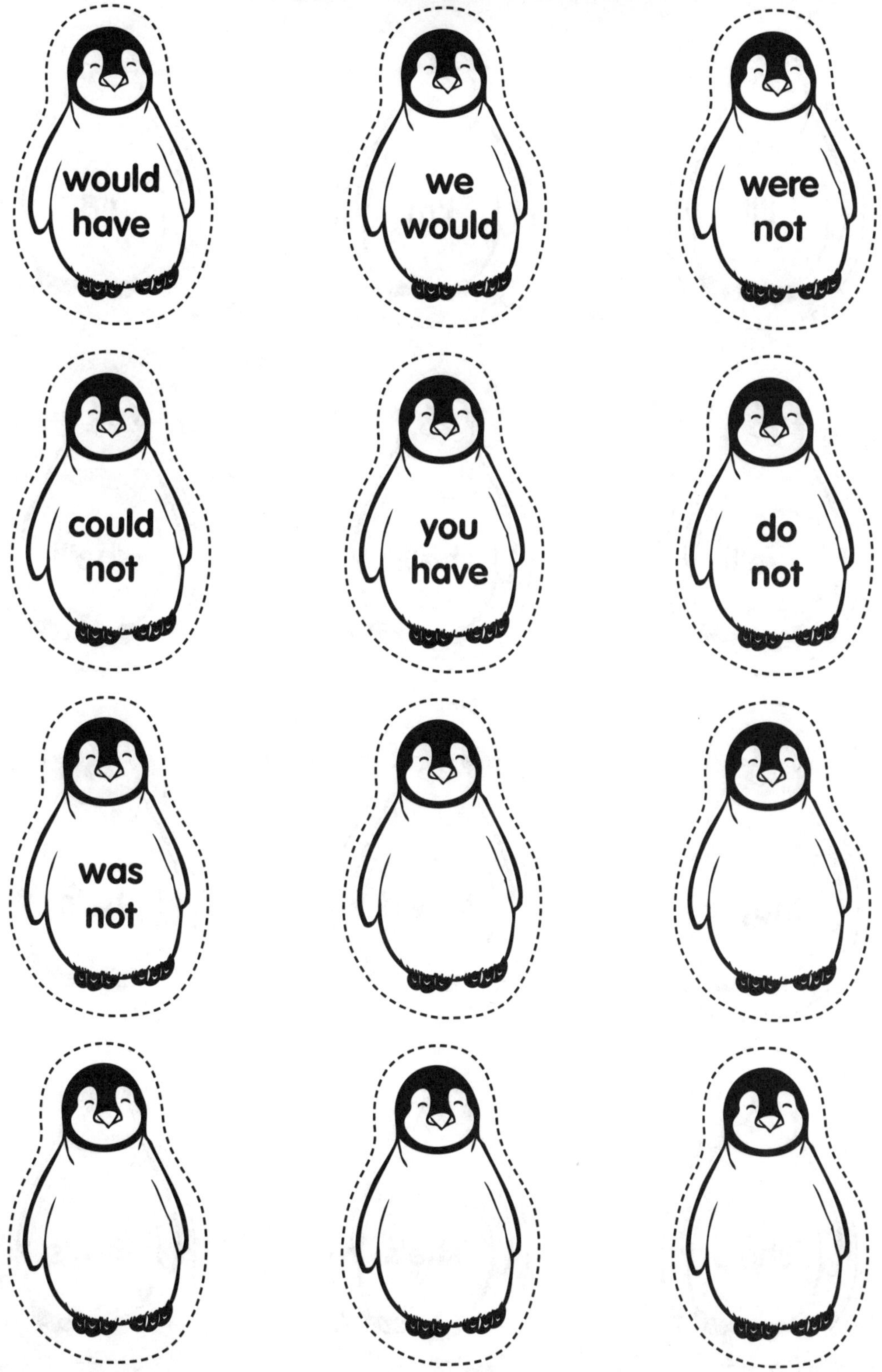
would have
we would
were not
could not
you have
do not
was not

Just Chilling

Contraction Game Pieces – 1

Cut out each
game piece.

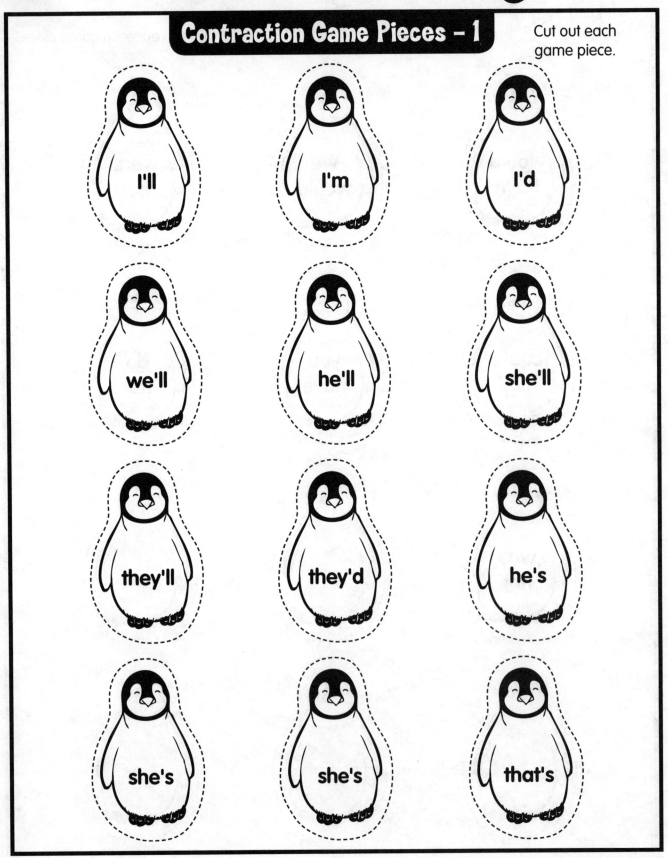

I'll

I'm

I'd

we'll

he'll

she'll

they'll

they'd

he's

she's

she's

that's

Match Mine: Primary
Kagan Publishing • 1 (800) 933-2667 • www.KaganOnline.com

Just Chilling

Contraction Game Pieces - 2

Cut out each game piece.

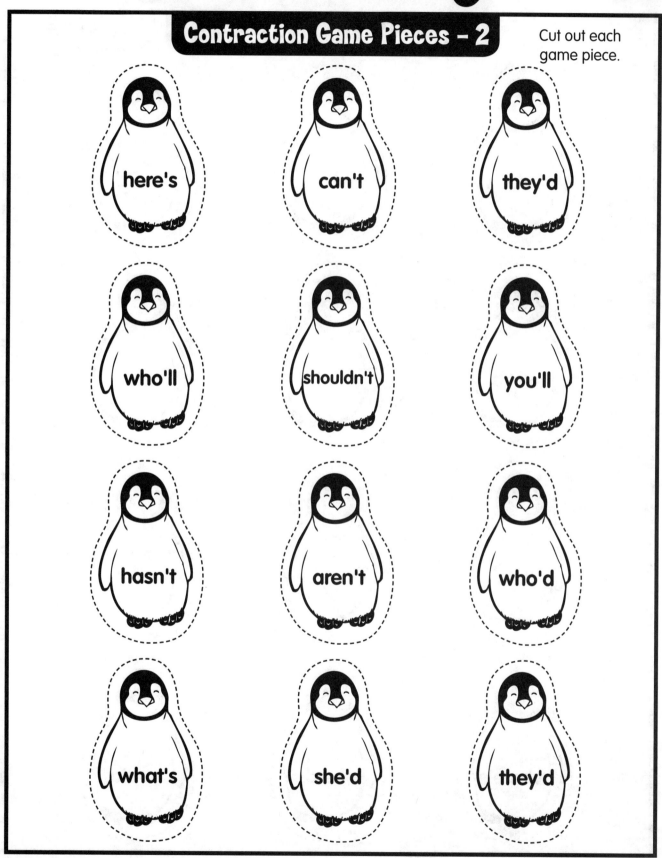

here's

can't

they'd

who'll

shouldn't

you'll

hasn't

aren't

who'd

what's

she'd

they'd

Just Chilling

Contraction Game Pieces – 3

Cut out each
game piece.

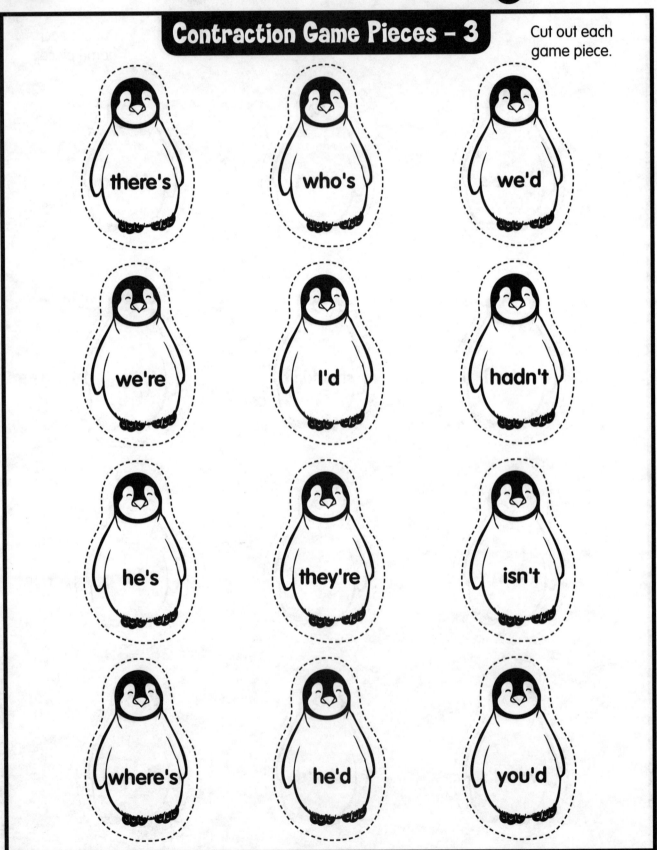

there's

who's

we'd

we're

I'd

hadn't

he's

they're

isn't

where's

he'd

you'd

Match Mine: Primary

Kagan Publishing • 1 (800) 933-2667 • www.KaganOnline.com

Just Chilling

Contraction Game Pieces – 4

Cut out each game piece.

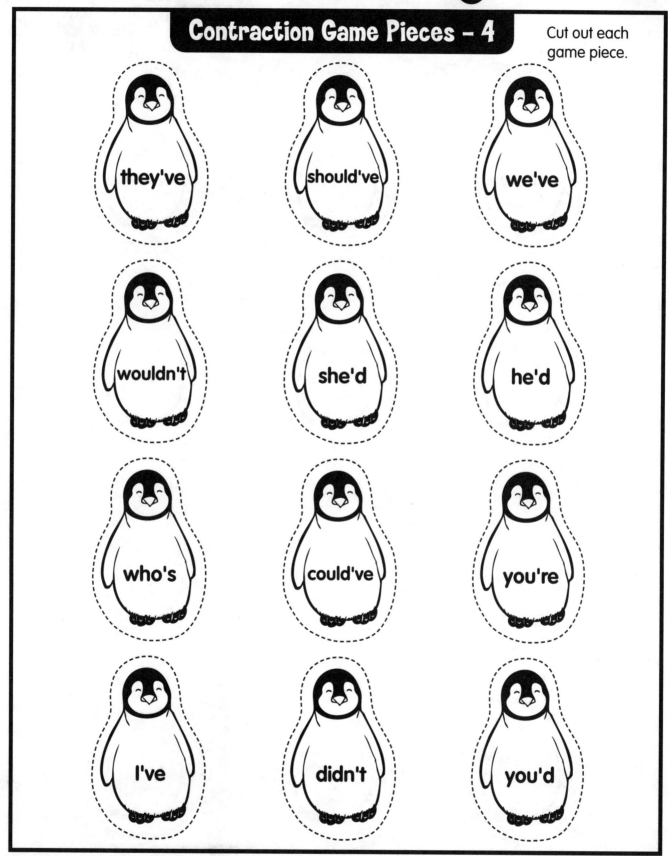

they've

should've

we've

wouldn't

she'd

he'd

who's

could've

you're

I've

didn't

you'd

Just Chilling

Contraction Game Pieces – 5

Cut out each game piece.

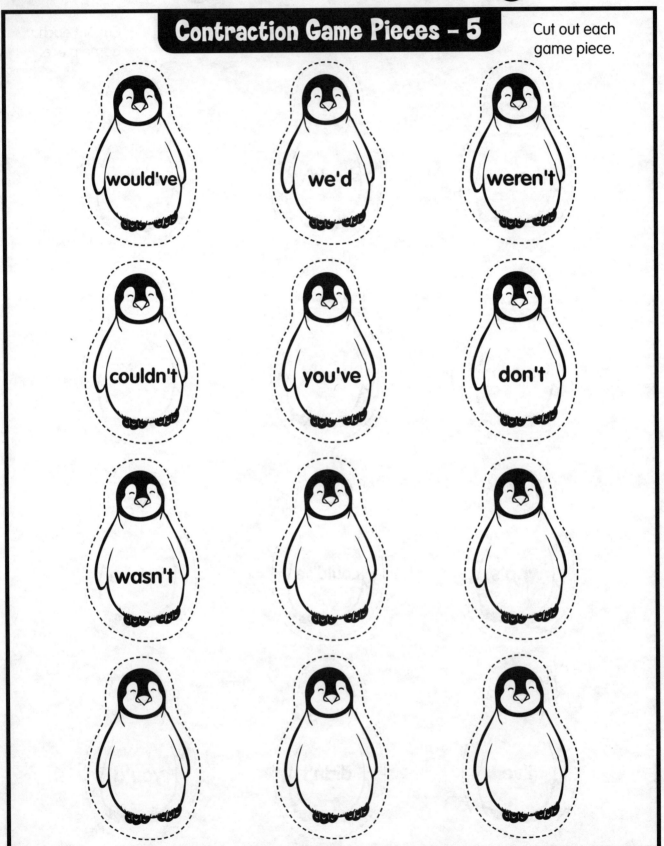

would've

we'd

weren't

couldn't

you've

don't

wasn't

Match Mine: Primary
Kagan Publishing • 1 (800) 933-2667 • www.KaganOnline.com

Landforms

Partner A sends one direction at a time, telling Partner B where to place the landform game piece on the Landforms game board. Partner B cooperates with Partner A to make a match.

Game Board

Game Pieces

Vocabulary

- Bottom
- Column
- Desert
- First
- Hills
- Island
- Lake
- Middle
- Mountain
- Plain
- Plateau
- River
- Row
- Second
- Third
- Top
- Valley

Common Core State Standards

MATH:
K.G.A.1 Describe objects in the environment using names of shapes, and describe the relative position of these objects using terms such as *above, below, beside, in front of, behind,* and *next to.*

SPEAKING & LISTENING:
COMPREHENSION AND COLLABORATION
SL.K.1a, SL.1.1a, SL.2.1a Follow agreed-upon rules for discussions.
SL.K.3, SL.1.3, SL.2.3 Ask and answer questions in order to seek help, get information, or clarify something that is not understood.

PRESENTATION OF KNOWLEDGE AND IDEAS
SL.K.6 Speak audibly and express thoughts, feelings, and ideas clearly.
SL.1.6, SL.2.6 Produce complete sentences when appropriate to task and situation.

Landforms

Match Mine: Primary

Kagan Publishing • 1 (800) 933-2667 • www.KaganOnline.com

Landforms

Game Pieces – Partner A

Cut out each
game piece.

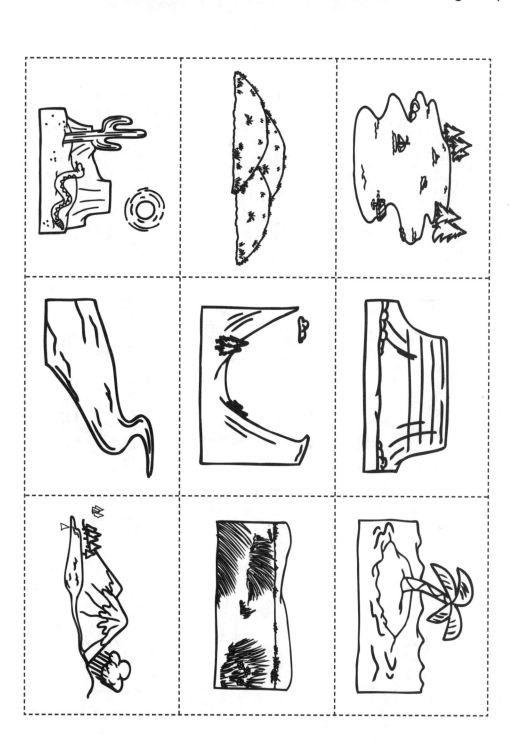

Landforms

Game Pieces – Partner B

Cut out each
game piece.

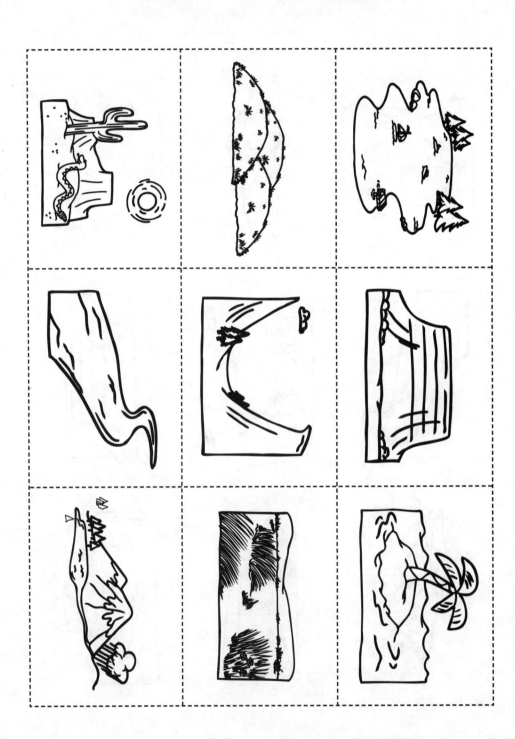

Match Mine: Primary
Kagan Publishing • 1 (800) 933-2667 • www.KaganOnline.com

Let It Grow

Partner A asks Partner B to find a word game piece that has the same vowel sound as the underlined sound and place it on a specific sunflower on the Let It Grow game board. Partner B cooperates with Partner A to make a match.

Game Board

Game Pieces

Vocabulary

- Baby
- Beanie
- Beans
- Bee
- Bike
- Book
- Boy
- Bread
- Cake
- Cherry
- Chief
- Claw
- Coat
- Coin
- Cry
- Doughnut
- Fruit
- Glue
- Gold
- Grass
- Hay
- House
- Key
- Knee
- Knight
- Owl
- Pen

- Petals
- Pie
- Plane
- Plate
- Pool
- Pull
- Rain
- Reindeer
- Rope
- Sausage
- School
- Shoe
- Sky
- Snail
- Snowman
- Soup
- Steak
- Stem
- Stew
- Sun
- Sunflower
- Team
- Toes
- Tooth
- Touch
- Weight

Common Core State Standards

MATH:
K.G.A.1 Describe objects in the environment using names of shapes, and describe the relative position of these objects using terms such as *above, below, beside, in front of, behind,* and *next to.*

READING:
FOUNDATIONAL SKILLS, PHONICS, AND WORD RECOGNITION
RF.2.3a Distinguish long and short vowels when reading regularly spelled one-syllable words.
RF.2.3b Know spelling-sound correspondences for additional common vowel teams.

Let It Grow

Let It Grow

Game Pieces – Partner A

Cut out each game piece.

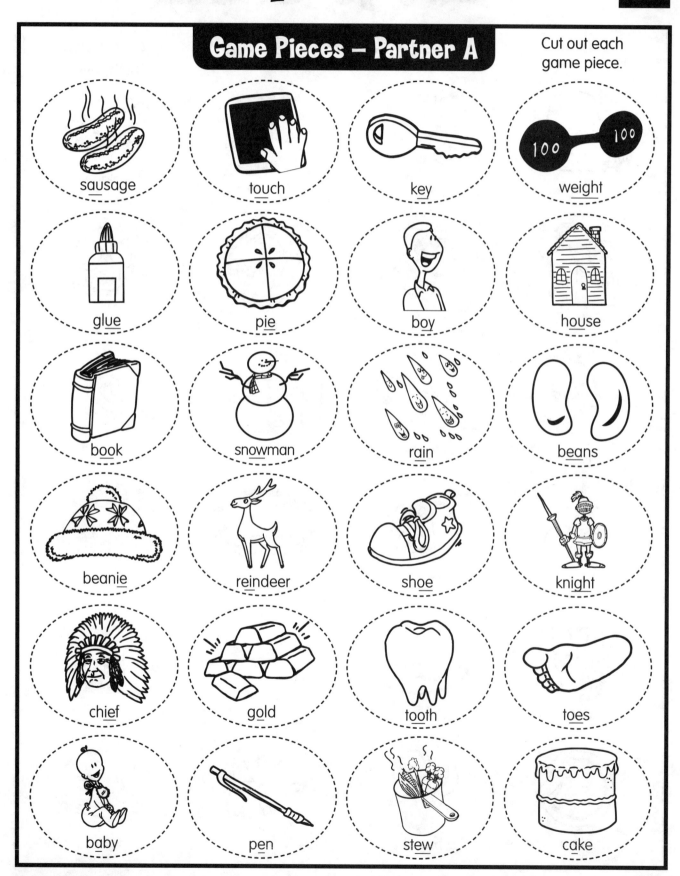

sausage

touch

key

weight

glue

pie

boy

house

book

snowman

rain

beans

beanie

reindeer

shoe

knight

chief

gold

tooth

toes

baby

pen

stew

cake

Let It Grow

Game Pieces – Partner B

Cut out each game piece.

claw

sun

team

plane

school

cry

coin

owl

pull

rope

hay

knee

cherry

snail

pool

bike

bee

doughnut

soup

coat

plate

bread

fruit

steak

Match Mine: Primary
Kagan Publishing • 1 (800) 933-2667 • www.KaganOnline.com

Mark The Spot

Partner A chooses the time on the digital clock and tells Partner B to find the corresponding time on the analog clock and place it on the ladybug on the Mark The Spot game board. Partner B cooperates with Partner A to make a match.

Vocabulary

- Analog clock
- Digital clock
- Half past
- Hour hand
- Minute hand
- O'clock
- Twelve o'clock
- Twelve thirty
- One o'clock
- One thirty
- Two o'clock
- Two thirty
- Three o'clock
- Three thirty
- Four o'clock
- Four thirty
- Five o'clock
- Five thirty
- Six o'clock
- Six thirty
- Seven o'clock
- Seven thirty
- Eight o'clock
- Eight thirty
- Nine o'clock
- Nine thirty
- Ten o'clock
- Ten thirty
- Eleven o'clock
- Eleven thirty

Game Board

Game Pieces

Common Core State Standards

MATH:
K.G.A.1 Describe objects in the environment using names of shapes, and describe the relative position of these objects using terms such as *above, below, beside, in front of, behind*, and *next to*.

MEASUREMENT AND DATA
1.MD.B.3 Tell and write time in hours and half-hours using analog and digital clocks.
2.MD.C.7 Tell and write time from analog and digital clocks to the nearest five minutes, using a.m. and p.m.

Mark The Spot

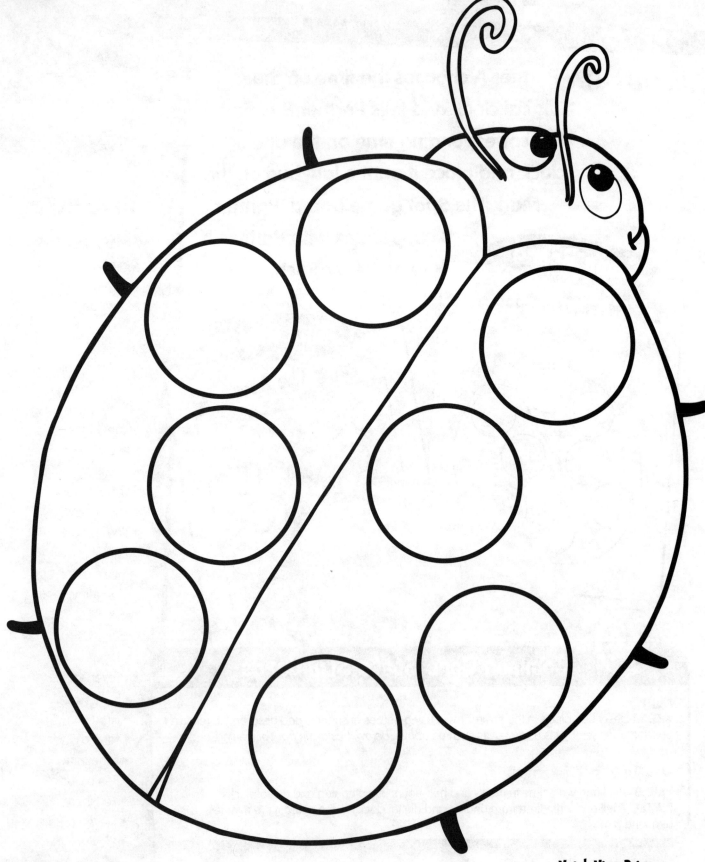

Match Mine: Primary
Kagan Publishing • 1 (800) 933-2667 • www.KaganOnline.com

Mark The Spot

Game Pieces – Partner A

Cut out each game piece.

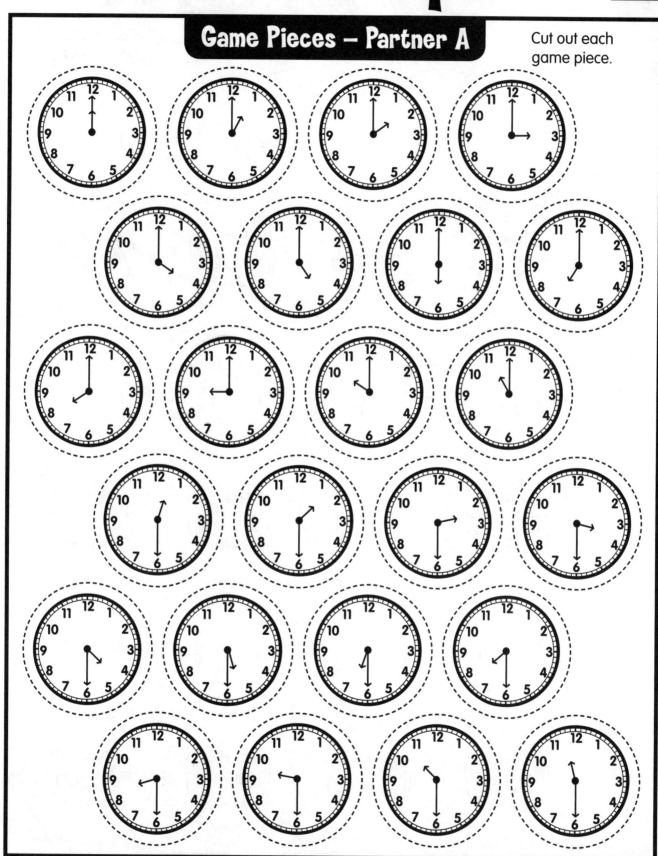

Mark The Spot

Game Pieces – Partner B

Cut out each game piece.

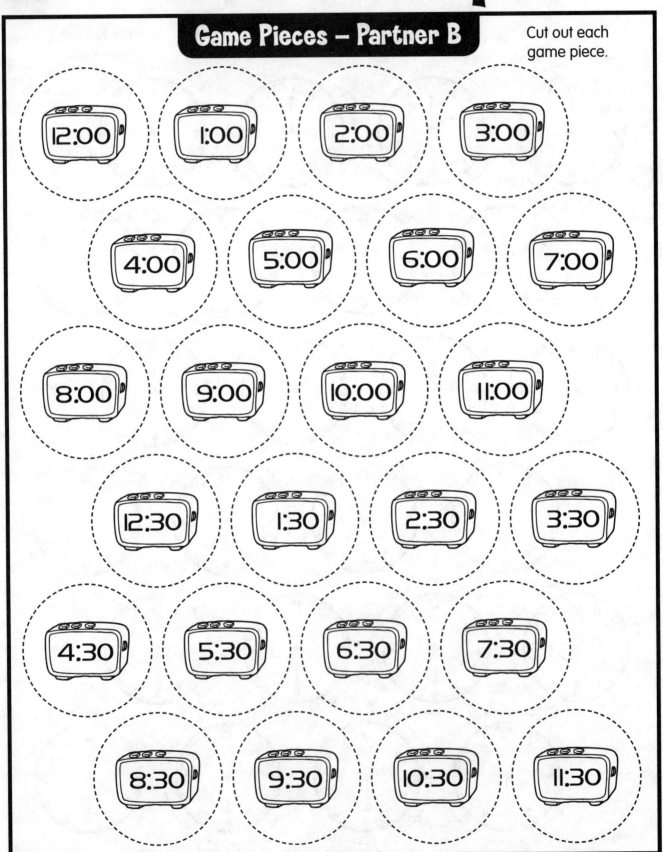

12:00   1:00   2:00   3:00

4:00   5:00   6:00   7:00

8:00   9:00   10:00   11:00

12:30   1:30   2:30   3:30

4:30   5:30   6:30   7:30

8:30   9:30   10:30   11:30

Match Mine: Primary
Kagan Publishing • 1 (800) 933-2667 • www.KaganOnline.com

Mark The Spot

Game Pieces – Blank Template

Cut out each game piece.

Mmmmm... Cookies

Partner A tells Partner B to place a plate of cookies, or a cookie with either a number, word, or fraction on the Mmmmm...... Cookie game board. Partner B cooperates with Partner A to make a match.

Game Board

Mmmmm... Cookies

Game Pieces

Mmmmm... Cookies
Cookie Game Pieces (1–12)
Cut out each game piece.

Differentiation

Differentiation is built into the game piece selection. Alternatives to having both the Sender and the Receiver having identical pieces are as follows. Sender has cookies with numerals and Receiver could have either a plate of cookies representing that number value or number words. Or, Sender has cookies partitioned into fractional pieces and Receiver has the fraction representing the partitioned cookies or the words representing those fractions.

Vocabulary

- Cookie jar
- Cookie sheet
- Cookies
- Eight
- Eighteen
- Eleven
- Fifteen
- Five
- Four
- Fourteen
- Fractions
- Nine
- Nineteen
- One
- One-fourth
- One-half
- One-quarter
- One-third
- Seven
- Seventeen
- Six
- Sixteen
- Ten
- Thirteen
- Three
- Three-quarters
- Twelve
- Twenty
- Two
- Two-fourths
- Two-quarters
- Two-thirds
- Whole numbers

Common Core State Standards

MATH:

K.G.A.1 Describe objects in the environment using names of shapes, and describe the relative position of these objects using terms such as *above, below, beside, in front of, behind*, and *next to*.

COUNTING & CARDINALITY:
KNOW NUMBER NAMES AND THE COUNT SEQUENCE
K.CC.A.1 Count to 100 by ones and by tens.

COUNT TO TELL THE NUMBER OF OBJECTS
K.CC.B.4 Understand the relationship between numbers and quantities; connect counting to cardinality.

K.CC.B.5 Count to answer "how many?" questions about as many as 20 things arranged in a line, a rectangular array, or a circle, or as many as 10 things in a scattered configuration; given a number from 1-20, count out that many objects.

Game 15

Mmmmm... Cookies

Match Mine: Primary
Kagan Publishing • 1 (800) 933-2667 • www.KaganOnline.com

Mmmmm... Cookies

Cookie Game Pieces (1–12)

Cut out each game piece.

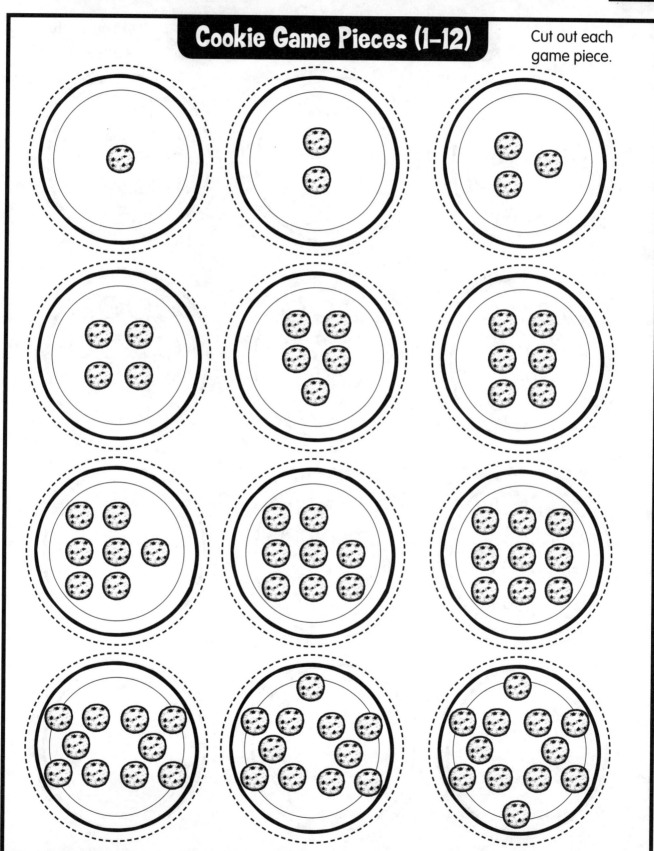

Mmmmm... Cookies

Cookie Game Pieces (13–20)

Cut out each game piece.

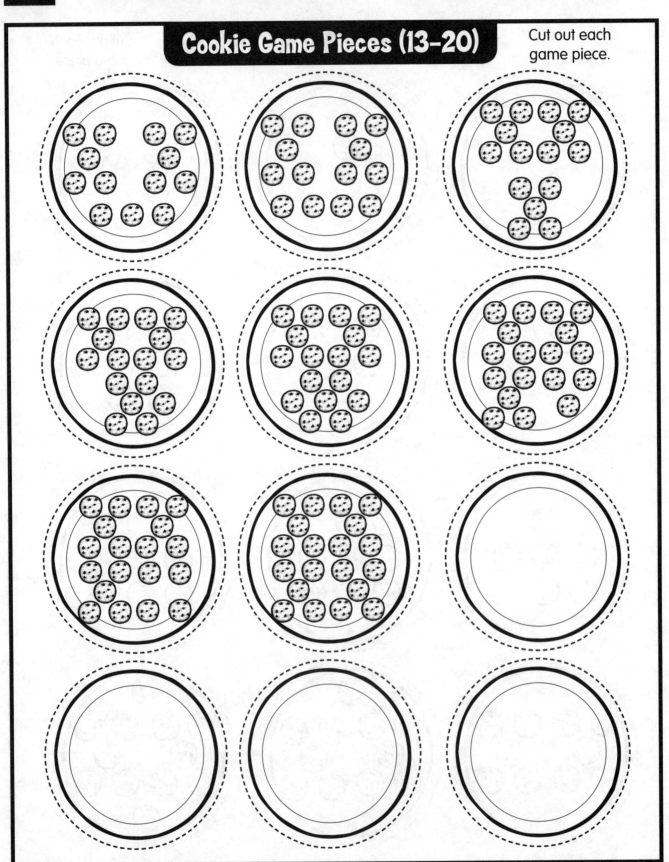

Match Mine: Primary
Kagan Publishing • 1 (800) 933-2667 • www.KaganOnline.com

Mmmmm... Cookies

Number Game Pieces (1–12)

Cut out each game piece.

1 2 3

4 5 6

7 8 9

10 11 12

Mmmmm... Cookies

Number Game Pieces (13–20)

Cut out each game piece.

Match Mine: Primary
Kagan Publishing • 1 (800) 933-2667 • www.KaganOnline.com

Mmmmmm... Cookies

Game 15

Word Game Pieces (One–Twelve)

Cut out each game piece.

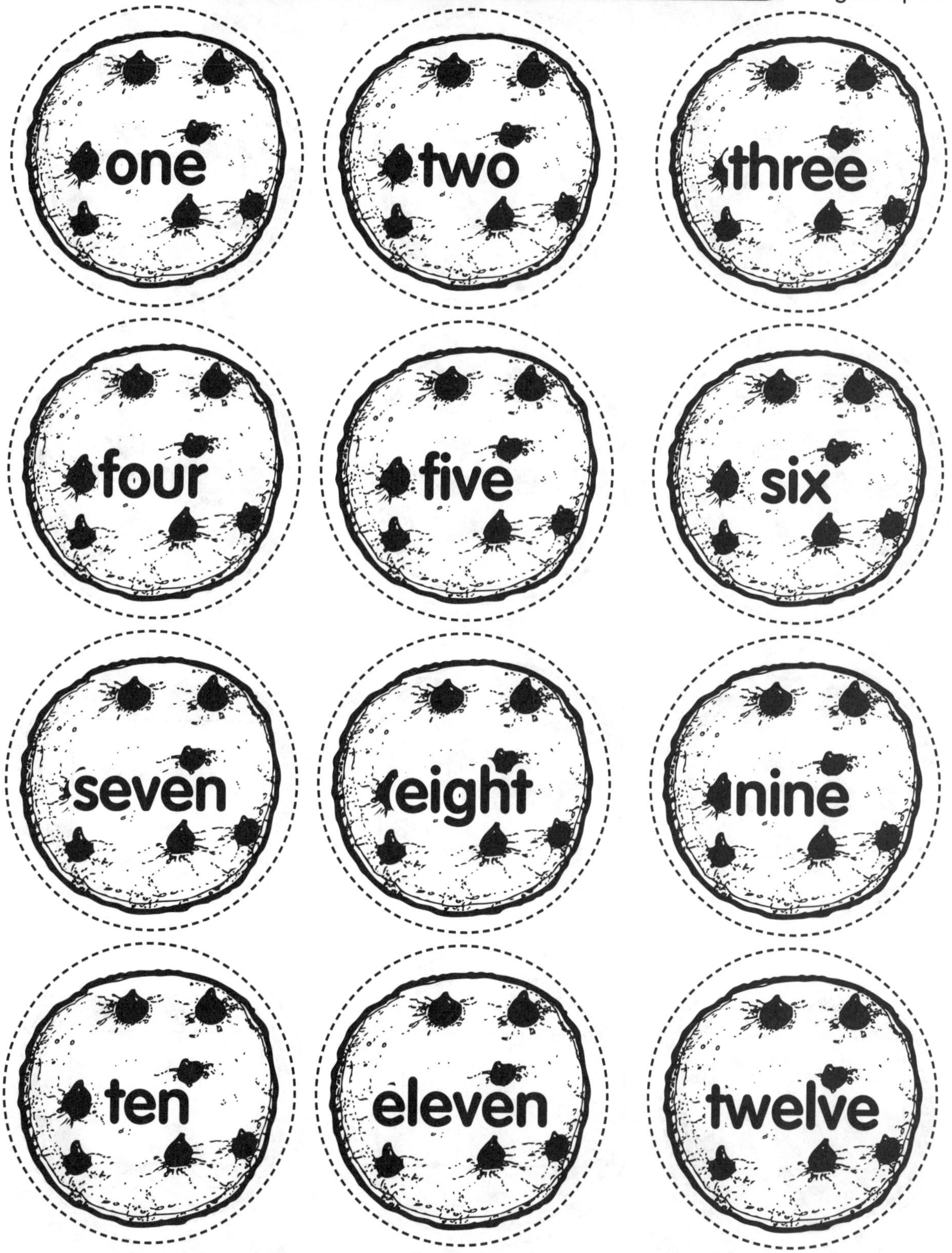
one
two
three
four
five
six
seven
eight
nine
ten
eleven
twelve

Mmmmm... Cookies

Cut out each game piece.

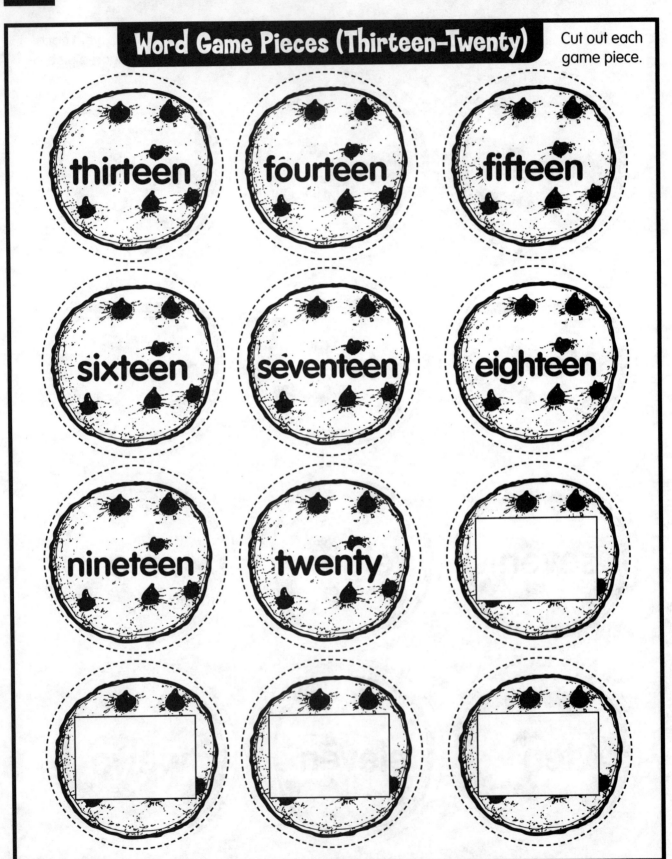

thirteen

fourteen

fifteen

sixteen

seventeen

eighteen

nineteen

twenty

Match Mine: Primary

Kagan Publishing • 1 (800) 933-2667 • www.KaganOnline.com

Mmmmm... Cookies

Fraction Game Pieces – Partner A

Cut out each game piece.

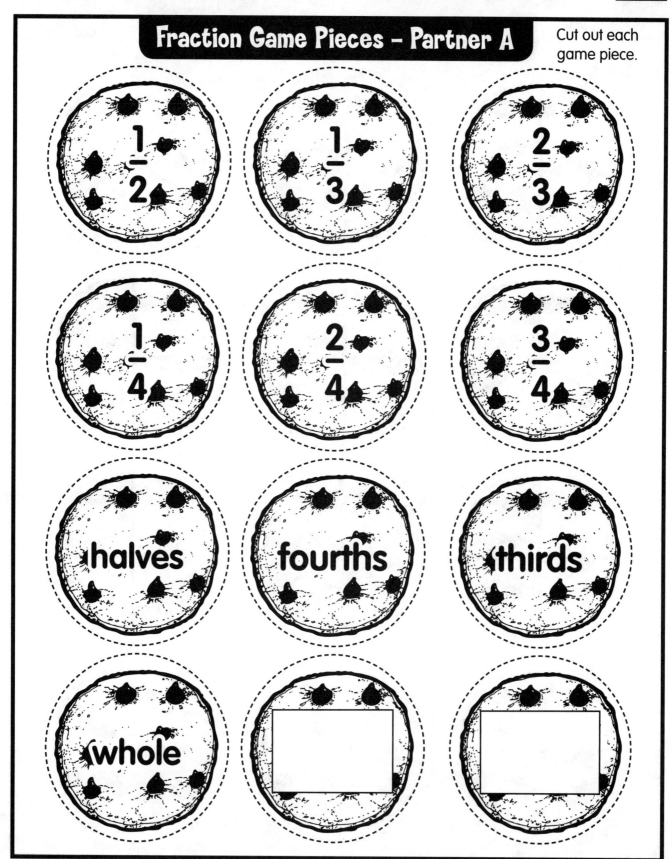

Mmmmm... Cookies

Fraction Game Pieces – Partner B

Cut out each
game piece.

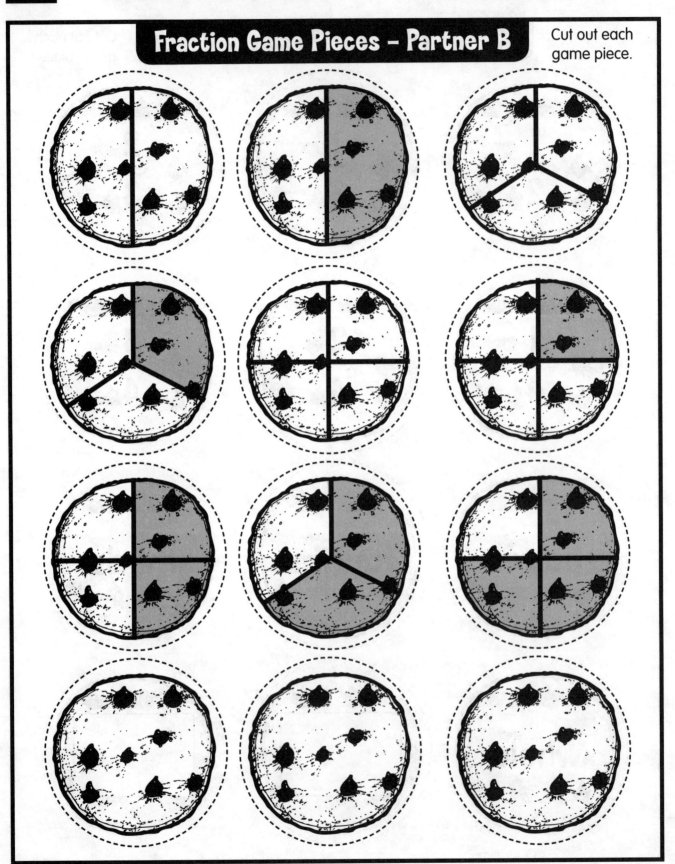

Mmmmm... Cookies

Fraction Game Pieces – Template

Cut out each game piece.

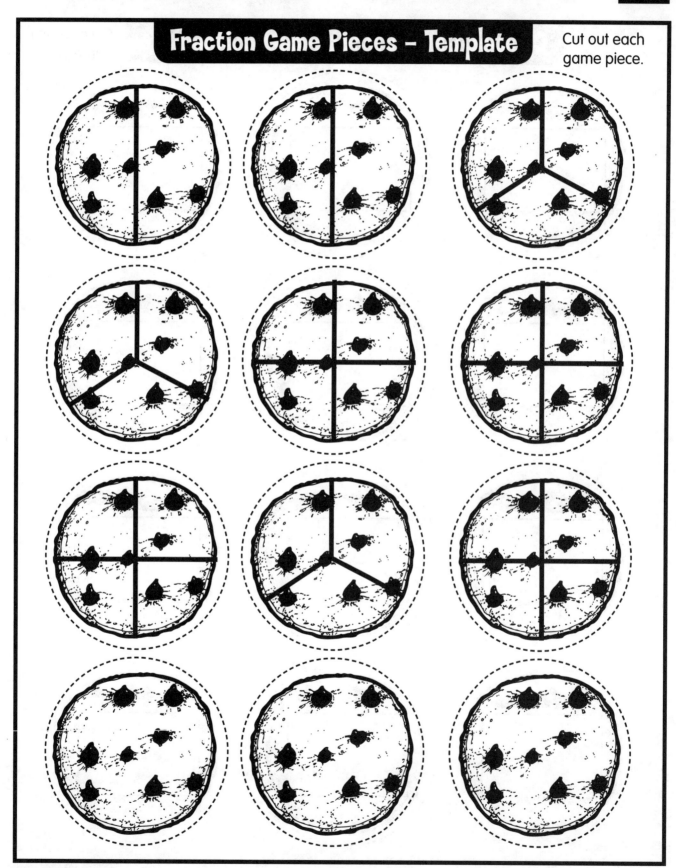

Mmmmm... Cookies

Cookies Game Pieces – Blank Template   Cut out each game piece.

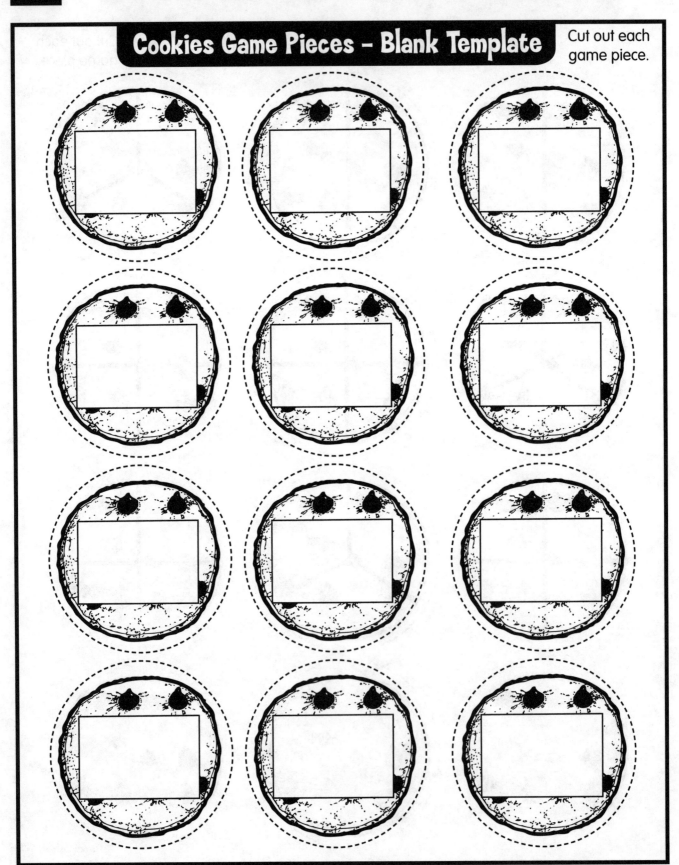

Match Mine: Primary
Kagan Publishing • 1 (800) 933-2667 • www.KaganOnline.com

On the Right Track

Partner A chooses the addition or subtraction game piece and tells Partner B to find the corresponding sum or difference and place it on the On the Right Track game board. Partner B cooperates with Partner A to make a match.

Game Board

Game 16 On the Right Track

Game Pieces

On the Right Track Game 16

Subtraction Game Pieces - 1

| 0 - 0 = | 1 - 0 = | 3 - 0 = | 5 - 0 = | Cut out each game piece. |

Kagan Publishing • 1 (800) 933-2667 • www.Kag...

Differentiation

So many options make this a great game to work on fluency of addition and subtraction facts. Your students can match addends to sums, addends to different addends that have the same sum, or an addition fact that equals a subtraction fact.

Vocabulary

- Above
- Add
- Addends
- Below
- Bottom
- Caboose
- Car
- Difference
- Engine
- Equals
- Fifth
- First
- Fourth
- Middle
- Minus
- Next
- Plus
- Second
- Subtract
- Sum
- Third
- Top

Common Core State Standards

MATH:
K.G.A.1 Describe objects in the environment using names of shapes, and describe the relative position of these objects using terms such as *above, below, beside, in front of, behind,* and *next to*.

OPERATIONS & ALGEBRAIC THINKING
K.OA.A.3 Decompose numbers less than or equal to 10 into pairs in more than one way.
K.OA.A.4 For any number from 1 to 9, find the number that makes 10 when added to the given number.
K.OA.A.5 Fluently add and subtract within 5.
1.OA.B.3 Apply properties of operations as strategies to add and subtract.
1.OA.C.6 Add and subtract within 20, demonstrating fluency for addition and subtraction within 10.
2.OA.B.2 Fluently add and subtract within 20 using mental strategies. By end of Grade 2, know from memory all sums of two 1-digit numbers.

On the Right Track

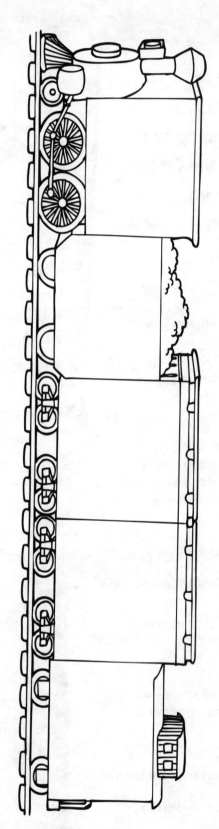

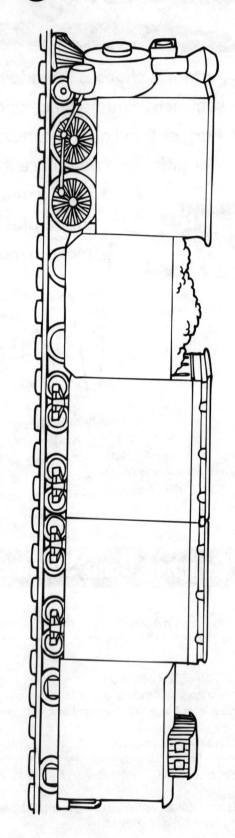

RIGHT TRACK

ON THE

On the Right Track

Subtraction Game Pieces –1

Cut out each game piece.

0 - 0 =	1 - 0 =	3 - 0 =	5 - 0 =
6 - 0 =	8 - 0 =	9 - 0 =	10 - 0 =
1 - 1 =	2 - 1 =	3 - 1 =	3 - 3 =
4 - 1 =	4 - 2 =	4 - 3 =	5 - 1 =
5 - 2 =	5 - 4 =	6 - 1 =	6 - 3 =
6 - 4 =	0 - 0 =	2 - 0 =	4 - 0 =
6 - 0 =	10 - 0 =	1 - 1 =	2 - 2 =
3 - 1 =	3 - 3 =	4 - 1 =	4 - 3 =

On the Right Track

Subtraction Game Pieces - 2

Cut out each
game piece.

5 - 0 =	5 - 1 =	5 - 2 =	5 - 4 =
5 - 5 =	6 - 1 =	6 - 3 =	6 - 6 =
7 - 0 =	7 - 5 =	7 - 7 =	8 - 2 =
8 - 4 =	8 - 6 =	8 - 7 =	9 - 0 =
9 - 2 =	9 - 5 =	10 - 1 =	10 - 3 =
10 - 5 =	10 - 10 =	11 - 4 =	11 - 8 =
11 - 10 =	11 - 11 =	12 - 4 =	12 - 7 =
12 - 8 =	12 - 9 =	12 - 10 =	12 - 12 =

Match Mine: Primary
Kagan Publishing • 1 (800) 933-2667 • www.KaganOnline.com

On the Right Track

Subtraction Answer Game Pieces - 1

Cut out each game piece.

0	1	3	5
6	8	9	10
0	1	2	0
3	2	1	4
3	1	5	3
2	0	2	4
6	10	0	0
2	0	3	1

On the Right Track

Subtraction Answer Game Pieces – 2

Cut out each
game piece.

5	4	3	1
0	5	3	0
7	2	0	6
4	2	1	9
7	4	9	7
5	0	7	3
1	0	8	5
4	3	2	0

Match Mine: Primary
Kagan Publishing • 1 (800) 933-2667 • www.KaganOnline.com

On the Right Track

Addition Game Pieces – 1

Cut out each game piece.

0 + 0 =	1 + 0 =	2 + 0 =	3 + 0 =
6 + 0 =	7 + 0 =	10 + 0 =	1 + 1 =
1 + 3 =	1 + 4 =	1 + 6 =	1 + 9 =
2 + 2 =	2 + 3 =	2 + 5 =	2 + 7 =
2 + 8 =	2 + 10 =	3 + 1 =	3 + 3 =
3 + 5 =	3 + 6 =	3 + 7 =	3 + 8 =
3 + 10 =	4 + 2 =	4 + 3 =	4 + 6 =
4 + 7 =	4 + 8 =	4 + 9 =	4 + 10 =

On the Right Track

Cut out each
game piece.

5 + 1 =	5 + 2 =	5 + 5 =	5 + 8 =
5 + 9 =	6 + 3 =	6 + 4 =	6 + 7 =
6 + 10 =	7 + 1 =	7 + 2 =	7 + 5 =
7 + 6 =	7 + 9 =	7 + 10 =	8 + 2 =
8 + 3 =	8 + 5 =	8 + 7 =	8 + 10 =
9 + 2 =	9 + 3 =	9 + 4 =	9 + 6 =
9 + 8 =	9 + 10 =	10 + 1 =	10 + 2 =
10 + 5 =	10 + 6 =	10 + 8 =	10 + 10 =

Match Mine: Primary
Kagan Publishing • 1 (800) 933-2667 • www.KaganOnline.com

On the Right Track

Addition Answer Game Pieces – 1

Cut out each game piece.

0	1	2	3
6	7	10	2
4	5	7	10
4	5	7	9
10	12	4	6
8	9	10	11
13	6	7	10
11	12	13	14

On the Right Track

6	7	10	13
14	9	10	13
16	8	9	12
13	16	17	10
11	13	15	18
11	12	13	15
17	19	11	12
15	16	18	20

Match Mine: Primary
Kagan Publishing • 1 (800) 933-2667 • www.KaganOnline.com

Pizza! Top It Off

Partner A chooses a fact family slice, then asks Partner B to find three matching number pepperoni pieces to place in the same location on the Pizza! Top It Off game board. Partner B cooperates with Partner A to make a match.

Vocabulary
- Addition
- Baker
- Equals
- Fact family
- Half
- Minus
- Pepperoni
- Pie
- Pizza
- Plus
- Slice
- Subtraction

Game Board

Pizza! Top It Off

Game Pieces

Pizza! Top It Off
Game Pieces 1 – Partner B

Cut out each game pieces.

1 1 1
1 2 2
2 3 3

Differentiation

This game can only be played with matching numbers on the pepperoni with matching numbers in the fact family; however, there are multiple fact family game pieces to choose from.

Common Core State Standards

MATH:
K.G.A.1 Describe objects in the environment using names of shapes, and describe the relative position of these objects using terms such as *above, below, beside, in front of, behind*, and *next to*.

OPERATIONS & ALGEBRAIC THINKING
K.OA.A.3 Decompose numbers less than or equal to 10 into pairs in more than one way.
1.OA.B.4 Understand subtraction as an unknown-addend problem.
1.OA.C.5 Relate counting to addition and subtraction.
2.OA.B.2 Fluently add and subtract within 20 using mental strategies. By end of Grade 2, know from memory all sums of two 1-digit numbers.

Pizza! Top It Off

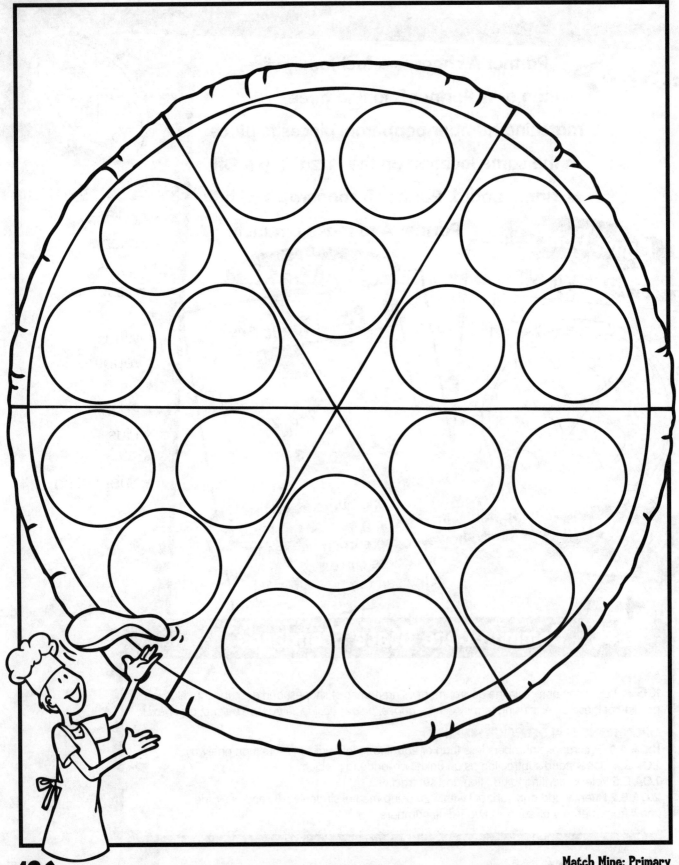

Pizza! Top It Off

Game Pieces 1 – Partner A

Cut out each game piece.

1 + 2 = 3
2 + 1 = 3
3 - 2 = 1
3 - 1 = 2

2 + 3 = 5
3 + 2 = 5
5 - 3 = 2
5 - 2 = 3

1 + 6 = 7
6 + 1 = 7
7 - 6 = 1
7 - 1 = 6

1 + 4 = 5
4 + 1 = 5
5 - 4 = 1
5 - 1 = 4

1 + 3 = 4
3 + 1 = 4
4 - 3 = 1
4 - 1 = 3

2 + 4 = 6
4 + 2 = 6
6 - 4 = 2
6 - 2 = 4

Pizza! Top It Off

Game Pieces 1 – Partner B

Cut out each game pieces.

1 1 1

1 2 2

2 3 3

3 4 4

4 5 5

6 6 7

Match Mine: Primary
Kagan Publishing • 1 (800) 933-2667 • www.KaganOnline.com

Pizza! Top It Off

Game Pieces 2 – Partner A

Cut out each game piece.

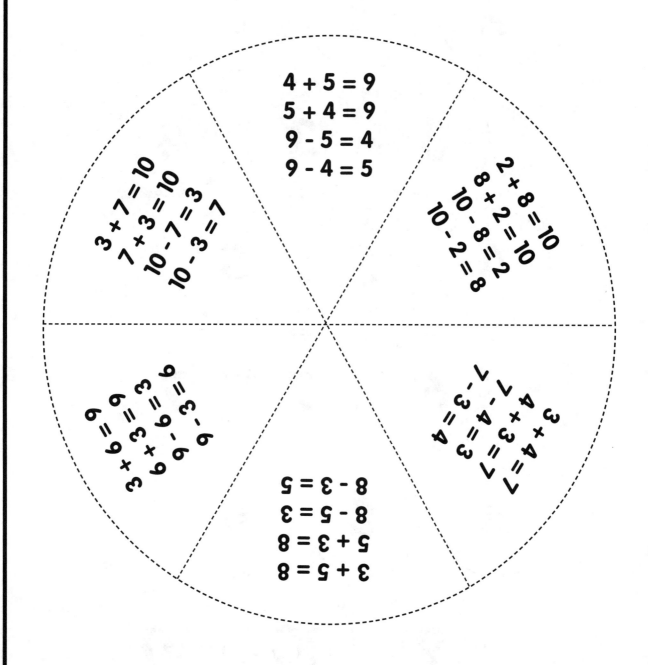

4 + 5 = 9
5 + 4 = 9
9 - 5 = 4
9 - 4 = 5

2 + 8 = 10
8 + 2 = 10
10 - 8 = 2
10 - 2 = 8

3 + 7 = 10
7 + 3 = 10
10 - 7 = 3
10 - 3 = 7

3 + 6 = 9
6 + 3 = 9
9 - 6 = 3
9 - 3 = 6

3 + 4 = 7
4 + 3 = 7
7 - 4 = 3
7 - 3 = 4

3 + 5 = 8
5 + 3 = 8
8 - 5 = 3
8 - 3 = 5

Pizza! Top It Off

Game Pieces 2 – Partner B

Cut out each game piece.

Match Mine: Primary
Kagan Publishing • 1 (800) 933-2667 • www.KaganOnline.com

Pizza! Top It Off

Game Pieces 3 – Partner A

Cut out each game piece.

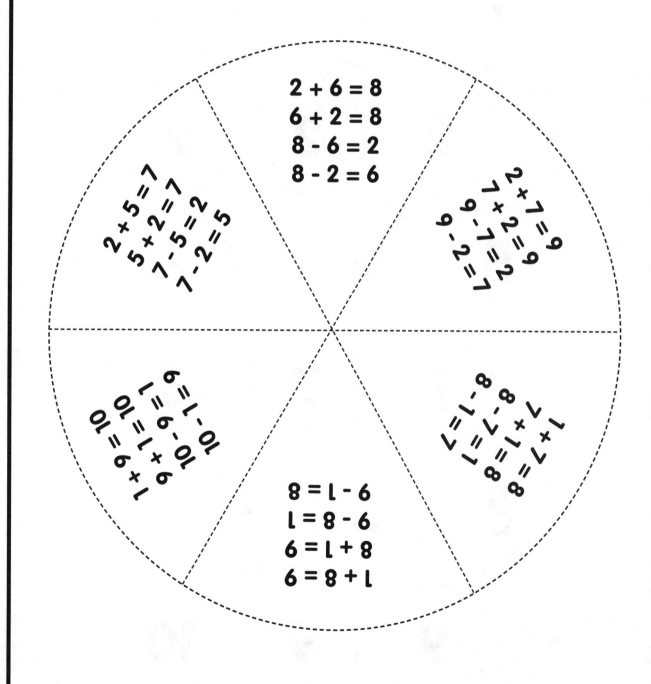

$$2 + 6 = 8$$
$$6 + 2 = 8$$
$$8 - 6 = 2$$
$$8 - 2 = 6$$

$$2 + 7 = 9$$
$$7 + 2 = 9$$
$$9 - 7 = 2$$
$$9 - 2 = 7$$

$$2 + 5 = 7$$
$$5 + 2 = 7$$
$$7 - 5 = 2$$
$$7 - 2 = 5$$

$$9 + 1 = 10$$
$$1 + 9 = 10$$
$$10 - 9 = 1$$
$$10 - 1 = 9$$

$$1 + 7 = 8$$
$$7 + 1 = 8$$
$$8 - 7 = 1$$
$$8 - 1 = 7$$

$$6 - 1 = 8$$
$$6 - 8 = 1$$
$$8 + 1 = 6$$
$$1 + 8 = 6$$

Pizza! Top It Off

Cut out each game piece.

Pizza! Top It Off

Game Pieces 4 – Partner A

Cut out each game piece.

$$4 + 9 = 13$$
$$9 + 4 = 13$$
$$13 - 9 = 4$$
$$13 - 4 = 9$$

$$4 + 6 = 10$$
$$6 + 4 = 10$$
$$10 - 6 = 4$$
$$10 - 4 = 6$$

$$4 + 8 = 12$$
$$8 + 4 = 12$$
$$12 - 8 = 4$$
$$12 - 4 = 8$$

$$5 + 6 = 11$$
$$6 + 5 = 11$$
$$11 - 6 = 5$$
$$11 - 5 = 6$$

$$4 + 7 = 11$$
$$7 + 4 = 11$$
$$11 - 7 = 4$$
$$11 - 4 = 7$$

$$5 + 7 = 12$$
$$7 + 5 = 12$$
$$12 - 7 = 5$$
$$12 - 5 = 7$$

Pizza! Top It Off

4 4 4

4 5 5

6 6 7

7 8 9

10 11 11

12 12 13

Pizza! Top It Off

Game Pieces 5 – Partner A

Cut out each game piece.

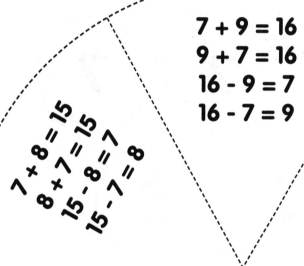
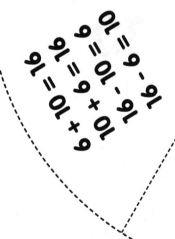

7 + 9 = 16
9 + 7 = 16
16 − 9 = 7
16 − 7 = 9

7 + 8 = 15
8 + 7 = 15
15 − 8 = 7
15 − 7 = 8

6 + 7 = 13
7 + 6 = 13
13 − 7 = 6
13 − 6 = 7

9 + 10 = 16
10 + 9 = 16
16 − 10 = 9
16 − 9 = 10

6 + 8 = 14
8 + 6 = 14
14 − 6 = 8
14 − 8 = 6

6 + 9 = 15
9 + 6 = 15
15 − 6 = 9
15 − 9 = 6

Pizza! Top It Off

Cut out each
game piece.

6 6 6

6 7 7

7 8 8

9 9 10

13 14 15

15 16 16

Match Mine: Primary
Kagan Publishing • 1 (800) 933-2667 • www.KaganOnline.com

Pizza! Top It Off

Game Pieces 6 – Partner A

Cut out each game piece.

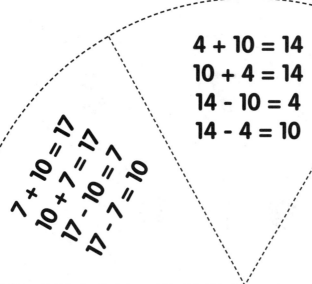

$$4 + 10 = 14$$
$$10 + 4 = 14$$
$$14 - 10 = 4$$
$$14 - 4 = 10$$

$$5 + 8 = 13$$
$$8 + 5 = 13$$
$$13 - 8 = 5$$
$$13 - 5 = 8$$

$$7 + 10 = 17$$
$$10 + 7 = 17$$
$$17 - 10 = 7$$
$$17 - 7 = 10$$

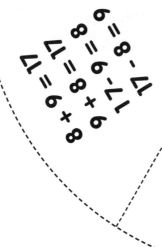

$$8 + 9 = 17$$
$$9 + 8 = 17$$
$$17 - 8 = 9$$
$$17 - 9 = 8$$

$$5 + 9 = 14$$
$$9 + 5 = 14$$
$$14 - 9 = 5$$
$$14 - 5 = 9$$

$$5 + 10 = 15$$
$$10 + 5 = 15$$
$$15 - 10 = 5$$
$$15 - 5 = 10$$

Pizza! Top It Off

Game Pieces 6 – Partner B

Cut out each game piece.

Match Mine: Primary
Kagan Publishing • 1 (800) 933-2667 • www.KaganOnline.com

Pizza! Top It Off

Game Pieces 7 – Partner A

Cut out each game piece.

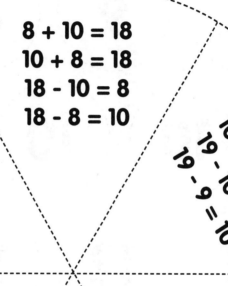

8 + 10 = 18
10 + 8 = 18
18 - 10 = 8
18 - 8 = 10

9 + 10 = 19
10 + 9 = 19
19 - 10 = 9
19 - 9 = 10

10 + 11 = 21
11 + 10 = 21
21 - 11 = 10
21 - 10 = 11

12 + 13 = 25
13 + 12 = 25
25 - 13 = 12
25 - 12 = 13

11 + 12 = 23
12 + 11 = 23
23 - 12 = 11
23 - 11 = 12

Pizza! Top It Off

Game Pieces 7 – Partner B

Cut out each game piece.

Match Mine: Primary
Kagan Publishing • 1 (800) 933-2667 • www.KaganOnline.com

Put It On the Shelf

Partner A tells Partner B to put a book with either a beginning letter or a toy on the bookcase on the Put It On the Shelf game board shelf. Partner B cooperates with Partner A to make a match.

Game Board

Game 18 Put It On the Shelf

Game Pieces

Put It On the Shelf

Game Pieces – Lower Case Letters   Game 18

Cut out each game piece.

a b c d e
f g h i j
k l m n o

Differentiation

Depending on the level of knowledge of letters and beginning sounds, you can choose the following scenarios: capital letters with matching lowercase letters; capital letters with matching pictures; or lowercase letters with matching pictures.

Common Core State Standards

READING:

FOUNDATIONAL SKILLS, PRINT CONCEPTS

RF.K.1b Recognize that spoken words are represented in written language by specific sequences of letters.

RF.K.1d Recognize and name all upper- and lowercase letters of the alphabet.

PHONOLOGICAL AWARENESS

RF.K.2d Isolate and pronounce the initial, medial vowel, and final sounds (phonemes) in three-phoneme words.

Vocabulary

- Alligator
- Ball
- Crab
- Dog
- Egg
- Frog
- Grape
- Heart
- Igloo
- Jam
- Key
- Leaf
- Letter names
- Letter sounds
- Moon
- Nail
- Owl
- Pig
- Question
- Rainbow
- Seal
- Shelf
- Truck
- Umbrella
- Volcano
- Worm
- X-ray
- Zebra

Put It On the Shelf

Match Mine: Primary
Kagan Publishing • 1 (800) 933-2667 • www.KaganOnline.com

Put It On the Shelf

Game Pieces – Lower Case Letters

Cut out each game piece.

a	b	c	d	e
f	g	h	i	j
k	l	m	n	o
p	q	r	s	t
u	v	w	x	y
z				

Put It On the Shelf

Cut out each game piece.

Put It On the Shelf

Game Pieces – Pictures

Cut out each game piece.

Rainforest Adventure

Partner A sends one direction at a time, telling Partner B where to place the rainforest animal on a specific part of the Rainforest Adventure game board: forest floor, understory, canopy, or emergent layer. Partner B cooperates with Partner A to make a match.

Game Board

Game Pieces

Vocabulary

- Anteater
- Branches
- Canopy
- Crocodile
- Emergent layer
- Forest floor
- Frog
- Jaguar
- Layer
- Leaves
- Lizard
- Monkey
- Parrot
- Roots
- Sloth
- Snake
- Toucan
- Trees
- Understory

Common Core State Standards

MATH:
K.G.A.1 Describe objects in the environment using names of shapes, and describe the relative position of these objects using terms such as *above, below, beside, in front of, behind,* and *next to.*

SPEAKING & LISTENING:
COMPREHENSION AND COLLABORATION
SL.K.1a, SL.1.1a, SL.2.1a Follow agreed-upon rules for discussions.
SL.K.3, SL.1.3, SL.2.3 Ask and answer questions in order to seek help, get information, or clarify something that is not understood.

PRESENTATION OF KNOWLEDGE AND IDEAS
SL.K.6 Speak audibly and express thoughts, feelings, and ideas clearly.
SL.1.6, SL.2.6 Produce complete sentences when appropriate to task and situation.

Rainforest Adventure

Emergent Layer

Canopy

Understory

Forest Floor

Match Mine: Primary

Kagan Publishing • 1 (800) 933-2667 • www.KaganOnline.com

Rainforest Adventure

Game Pieces – Partner A

Cut out each game piece.

Game Pieces – Partner B

Cut out each game piece.

Partner A chooses a game piece, then asks Partner B to find the same game piece and place it on the Reach for the Stars game board. Partner B cooperates with Partner A to make a match.

Game Board

Game 20 — Reach for the Stars

Game Pieces

Reach for the Stars — Space Game Pieces – Partner A — Game 20 — Cut out each game piece.

Differentiation

This game can be played with either matching Space game pieces or matching Phases of the Moon game pieces.

Vocabulary

- Astronaut
- Big Dipper
- Earth
- First quarter
- Full moon
- Jupiter
- Last quarter
- Mars
- Mars Rover
- Mercury
- Milky Way
- Moon
- Neptune
- New moon
- Ozone layer
- Saturn
- Shooting star
- Space shuttle
- Stars
- Sun
- Uranus
- Venus
- Waning crescent
- Waxing crescent
- Waning gibbous
- Waxing gibbous

Common Core State Standards

MATH:
K.G.A.1 Describe objects in the environment using names of shapes, and describe the relative position of these objects using terms such as *above, below, beside, in front of, behind,* and *next to.*

SPEAKING & LISTENING:
COMPREHENSION AND COLLABORATION
SL.K.1a, SL.1.1a, SL.2.1a Follow agreed-upon rules for discussions.
SL.K.3, SL.1.3, SL.2.3 Ask and answer questions in order to seek help, get information, or clarify something that is not understood.

PRESENTATION OF KNOWLEDGE AND IDEAS
SL.K.6 Speak audibly and express thoughts, feelings, and ideas clearly.
SL.1.6, SL.2.6 Produce complete sentences when appropriate to task and situation.

Reach for the Stars

Match Mine: Primary
Kagan Publishing • 1 (800) 933-2667 • www.KaganOnline.com

Reach for the Stars

Space Game Pieces – Partner A

Cut out each
game piece.

Earth

Mars

Moon

Saturn

Venus

Jupiter

Neptune

Mercury

Uranus

Sun

Astronaut

Shooting Star

Space Shuttle

Mars Rover

Ozone Layer
OZONE
Layer

Big Dipper

Milky Way

Reach for the Stars

Space Game Pieces – Partner B

Cut out each game piece.

Earth
Mars
Moon
Saturn
Venus
Jupiter
Neptune
Mercury
Uranus
Sun
Shooting Star
Space Shuttle
Astronaut
Mars Rover
Ozone Layer
OZONE
Layer
Big Dipper
Milky Way

Match Mine: Primary
Kagan Publishing • 1 (800) 933-2667 • www.KaganOnline.com

Reach for the Stars

Phases of the Moon Game Pieces – Partner A

Cut out each game piece.

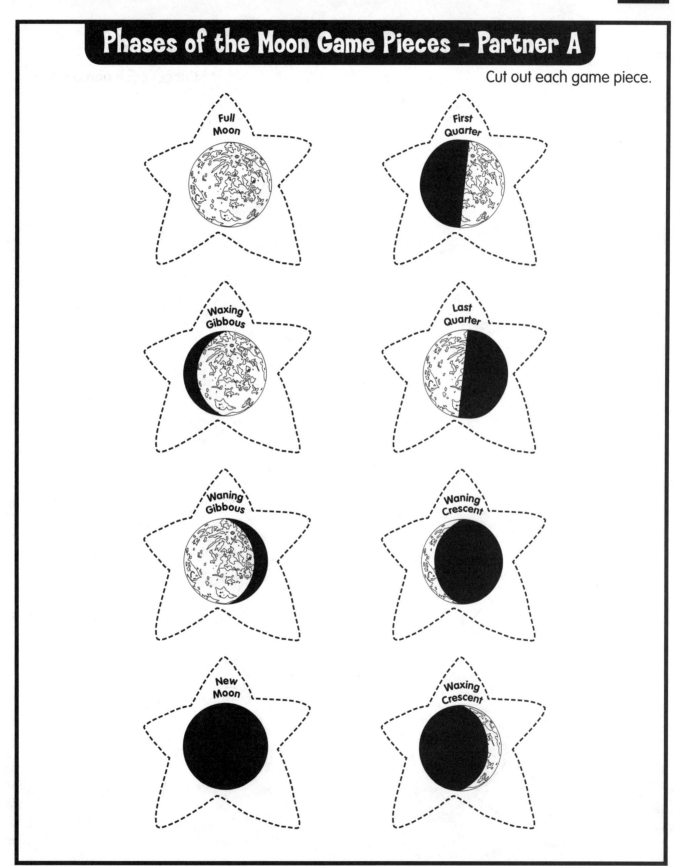

Reach for the Stars

Phases of the Moon Game Pieces – Partner B

Cut out each game piece.

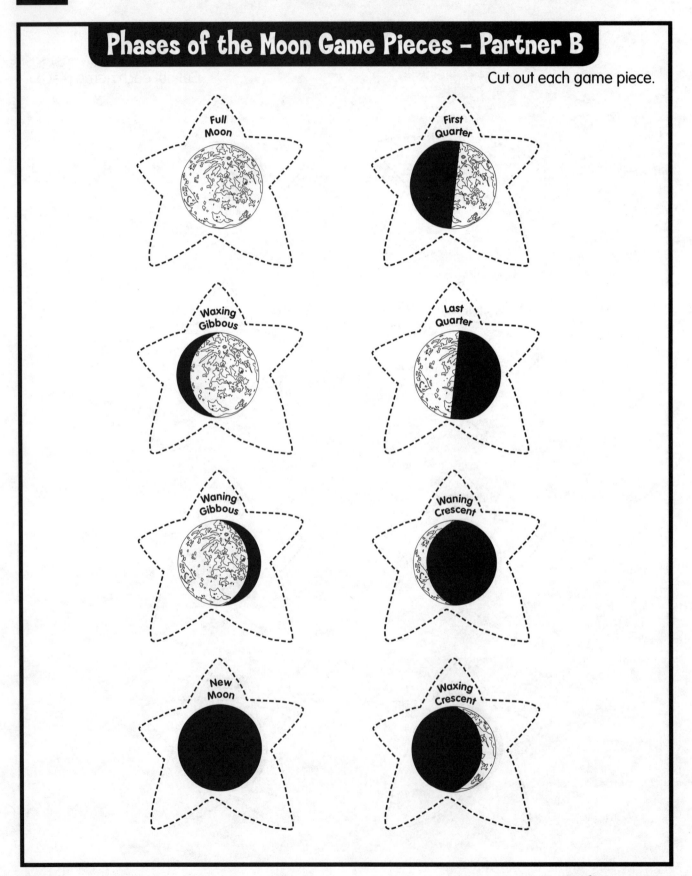

Full Moon

First Quarter

Waxing Gibbous

Last Quarter

Waning Gibbous

Waning Crescent

New Moon

Waxing Crescent

Match Mine: Primary
Kagan Publishing • 1 (800) 933-2667 • www.KaganOnline.com

Rope It

Partner A sends one direction at a time, telling Partner B where to place the Rope It game piece on the Rope It game board. Partner B cooperates with Partner A to make a match.

Game Board
Rope It

Game Pieces
Rope It
Game Pieces – Partner A

Vocabulary
- Above
- Bandana
- Below
- Beside
- Cactus
- Cowboy
- Cowboy boot
- Cowboy hat
- Cowgirl
- Coyote
- Donkey
- Horse
- Inside
- Miner
- Outside
- Rope
- Wagon

Common Core State Standards

MATH:
K.G.A.1 Describe objects in the environment using names of shapes, and describe the relative position of these objects using terms such as *above, below, beside, in front of, behind,* and *next to.*

SPEAKING & LISTENING:
COMPREHENSION AND COLLABORATION
SL.K.1a, SL.1.1a, SL.2.1a Follow agreed-upon rules for discussions.
SL.K.3, SL.1.3, SL.2.3 Ask and answer questions in order to seek help, get information, or clarify something that is not understood.

PRESENTATION OF KNOWLEDGE AND IDEAS
SL.K.6 Speak audibly and express thoughts, feelings, and ideas clearly.
SL.1.6, SL.2.6 Produce complete sentences when appropriate to task and situation.

Rope It

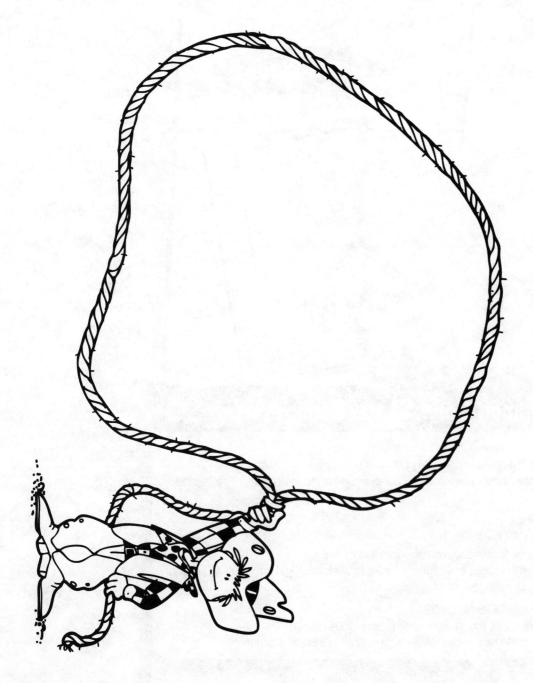

Match Mine: Primary
Kagan Publishing • 1 (800) 933-2667 • www.KaganOnline.com

Rope It

Game Pieces – Partner A

Cut out each game piece.

Rope It

Game Pieces – Partner B

Cut out each
game piece.

Match Mine: Primary
Kagan Publishing • 1 (800) 933-2667 • www.KaganOnline.com

Scarecrow

Partner A sends one direction at a time, telling Partner B where to place the Scarecrow game pieces on the Scarecrow game board. Partner B cooperates with Partner A to make a match.

Vocabulary

- Barn
- Black
- Fence
- Fifth
- First
- Fourth
- Grass
- Hat
- Hay
- Overalls
- Patch
- Scarecrow
- Second
- Shirt
- Solid
- Striped
- Third
- White

Common Core State Standards

MATH:
K.G.A.1 Describe objects in the environment using names of shapes, and describe the relative position of these objects using terms such as *above, below, beside, in front of, behind,* and *next to.*

SPEAKING & LISTENING:
COMPREHENSION AND COLLABORATION
SL.K.1a, SL.1.1a, SL.2.1a Follow agreed-upon rules for discussions.
SL.K.3, SL.1.3, SL.2.3 Ask and answer questions n order to seek help, get information, or clarify something that is not understood.

PRESENTATION OF KNOWLEDGE AND IDEAS
SL.K.6 Speak audibly and express thoughts, feelings, and ideas clearly.
SL.1.6, SL.2.6 Produce complete sentences when appropriate to task and situation.

Scarecrow

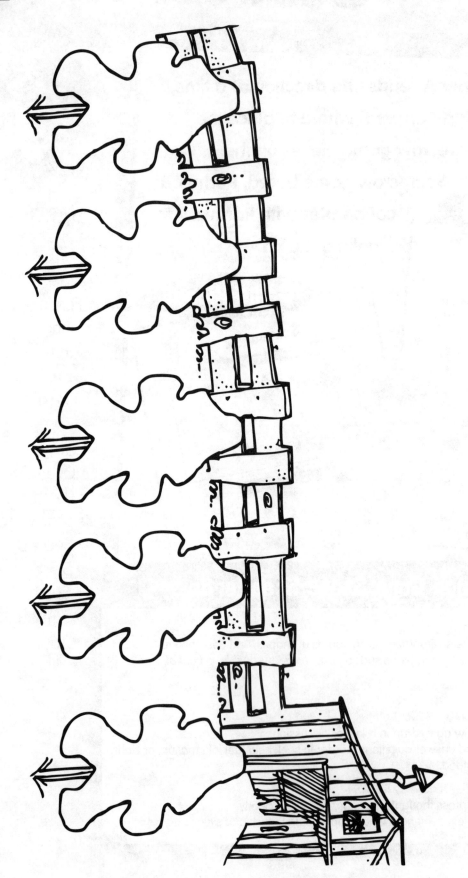

Scarecrow

Game Pieces – Partner A
Cut out each scarecrow.

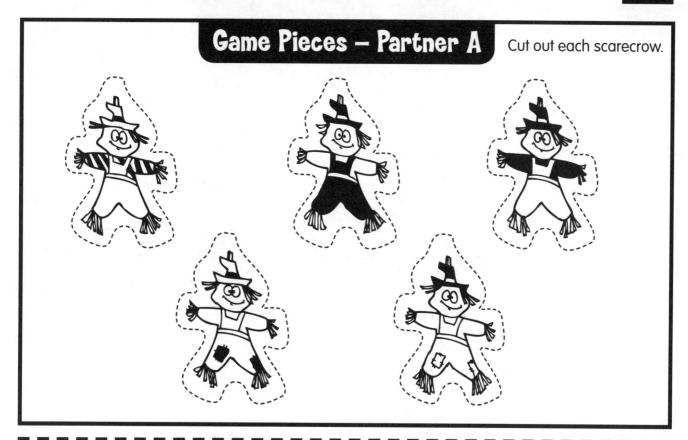

Game Pieces – Partner B
Cut out each scarecrow.

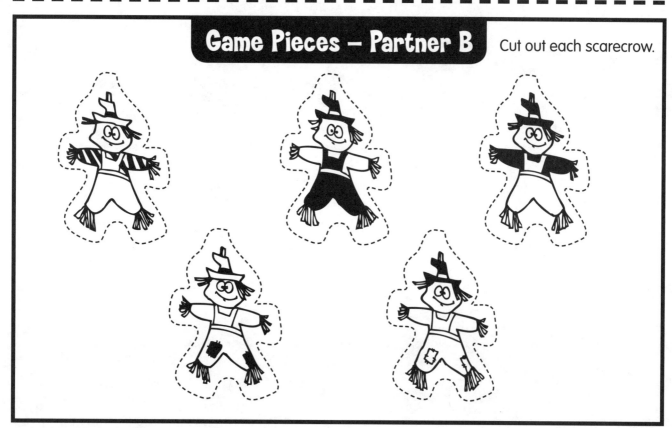

Shape Up

Partner A chooses a middle sound game piece, then asks Partner B to choose a picture game piece with the corresponding middle sound and place them on the Shape Up game board. Partner B cooperates with Partner A to make a match.

Vocabulary

- Bat
- Bell
- Bus
- Circle
- Dog
- Duck
- Fan
- Fish
- Heart
- Hexagon
- Lip
- Lock
- Map
- Mop
- Net
- Pen
- Pig
- Rectangle
- Rhombus
- Star
- Square
- Sun
- Trapezoid
- Triangle

Game Board
Shape Up

Game Pieces
Shape Up
Game Pieces – Partner B

Common Core State Standards

READING:
FOUNDATIONAL SKILLS, PHONICS, AND WORD RECOGNITION
RF.K.3, RF.1.3, RF.2.3 Know and apply grade-level phonics and word analysis skills in decoding words.
RF.K.3c Read common high-frequency words by sight.

FLUENCY
RF.K.4 Read emergent-reader texts with purpose and understanding.
RF.1.4, RF.2.4 Read with sufficient accuracy and fluency to support comprehension.

MATH:
K.G.A.1 Describe objects in the environment using names of shapes, and describe the relative position of these objects using terms such as *above, below, beside, in front of, behind,* and *next to.*

Shape Up

Match Mine: Primary
Kagan Publishing • 1 (800) 933-2667 • www.KaganOnline.com

Shape Up

Game Pieces – Partner A

Cut out each middle sound game piece.

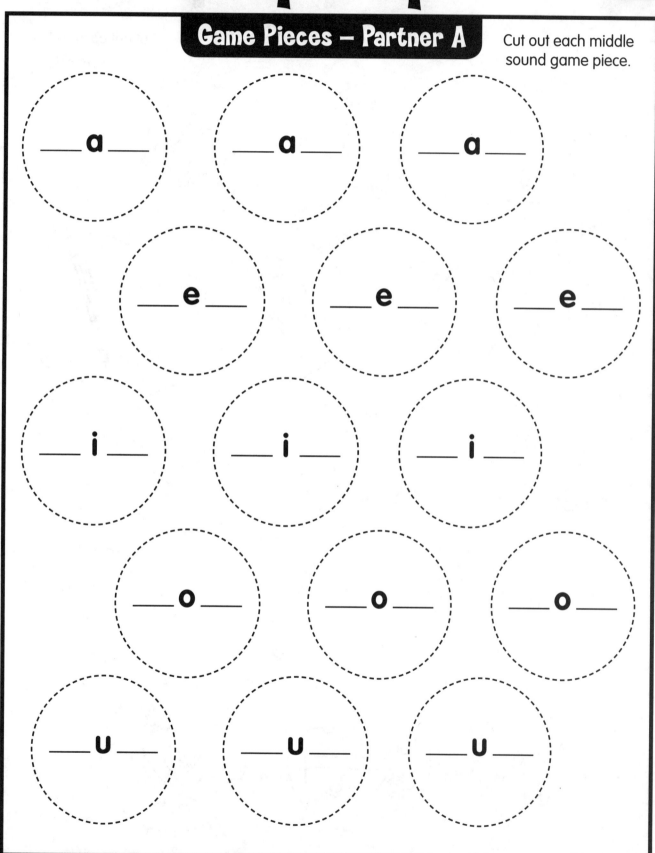

__a__   __a__   __a__

__e__   __e__   __e__

__i__   __i__   __i__

__o__   __o__   __o__

__u__   __u__   __u__

Shape Up

Game Pieces – Partner B

Cut out each picture
game piece.

Match Mine: Primary
Kagan Publishing • 1 (800) 933-2667 • www.KaganOnline.com

Partner A sends one direction at a time, telling Partner B where to place the Snowman game pieces on the Snowman game board. Partner B cooperates with Partner A to make a match.

Game Board

Game Pieces

Vocabulary

- Baseball cap
- Beanie hat
- Bottom
- Bow tie
- Buttons
- Carrot
- Coat
- Eyes
- Gloves
- Hand
- Hat
- Large
- Medium
- Middle
- Mouth
- Nose
- Pocket
- Scarf
- Small
- Snowman
- Top
- Twig

Common Core State Standards

MATH:
K.G.A.1 Describe objects in the environment using names of shapes, and describe the relative position of these objects using terms such as *above, below, beside, in front of, behind*, and *next to*.

SPEAKING & LISTENING:
COMPREHENSION AND COLLABORATION
SL.K.1a, SL.1.1a, SL.2.1a Follow agreed-upon rules for discussions.
SL.K.3, SL.1.3, SL.2.3 Ask and answer questions in order to seek help, get information, or clarify something that is not understood.

PRESENTATION OF KNOWLEDGE AND IDEAS
SL.K.6 Speak audibly and express thoughts, feelings, and ideas clearly.
SL.1.6, SL.2.6 Produce complete sentences when appropriate to task and situation.

Snowman

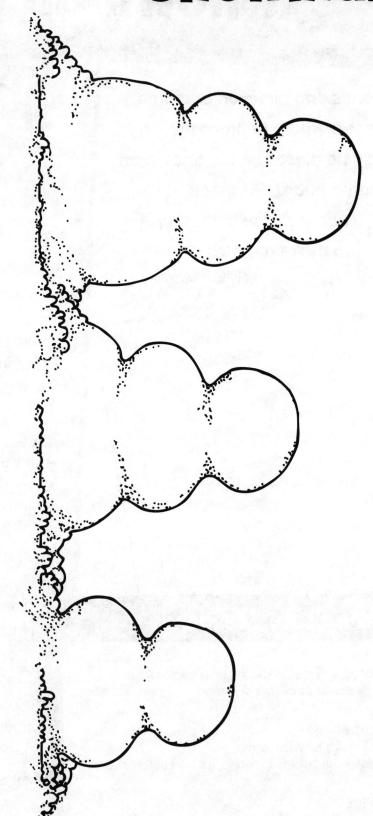

Match Mine: Primary
Kagan Publishing • 1 (800) 933-2667 • www.KaganOnline.com

Snowman

Game Pieces – Partner A

Cut out each game piece.

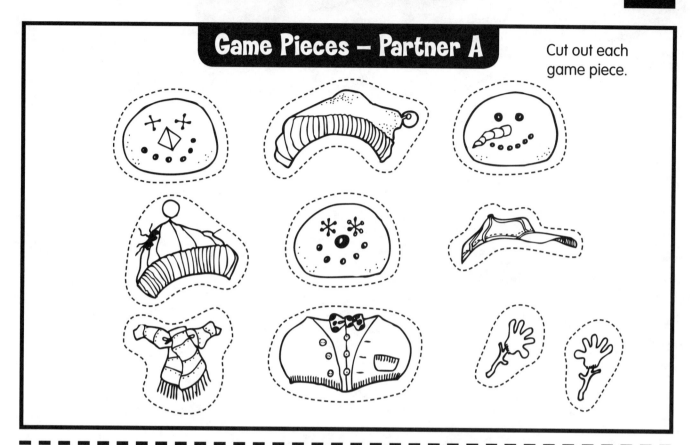

Game Pieces – Partner B

Cut out each game piece.

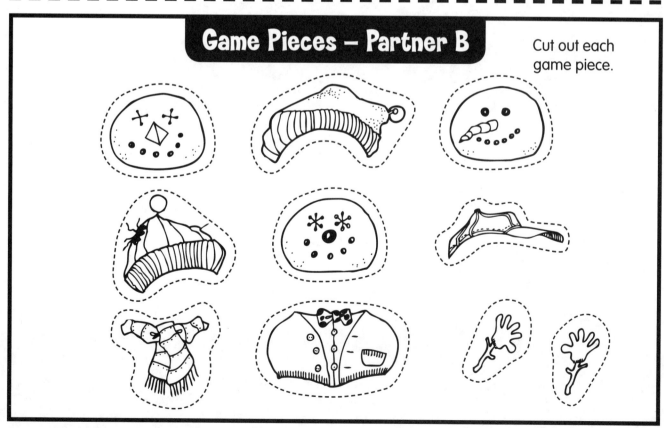

String Beads

Partner A asks Partner B to find an environmental object to match a 2D or 3D shape and tells Partner B where to place that shape on the String Beads game board. Partner B cooperates with Partner A to make a match.

Vocabulary

- 3D heart
- 3D star
- Badge
- Ball
- Bee
- Box of chocolates
- Calculator
- Candy jar
- Circle
- Clock
- Cube
- Cuboid (rectangle)
- Diamond
- Die
- Eraser
- Heart
- Hexagon
- Hexahedron
- Honeycomb
- Kite
- Octagon
- Octagonal Prism
- Parallelogram
- Penny
- Playing card
- Pyramid
- Rectangle
- Rhombus
- Sphere
- Square
- Stamp
- Star
- Starfish
- Stop sign
- Three-dimension
- Triangle
- Triangular prism
- Two-dimension

Game Board

Game Pieces

Differentiation

For an easier game, use the 2D shape set. To increase difficulty, use the 3D shape set.

Common Core State Standards

MATH:
GEOMETRY
K.G.A.1 Describe objects in the environment using names of shapes, and describe the relative position of these objects using terms such as *above, below, beside, in front of, behind,* and *next to.*

String Beads

Match Mine: Primary
Kagan Publishing • 1 (800) 933-2667 • www.KaganOnline.com

String Beads

2D Game Pieces – Partner A

Cut out each game piece.

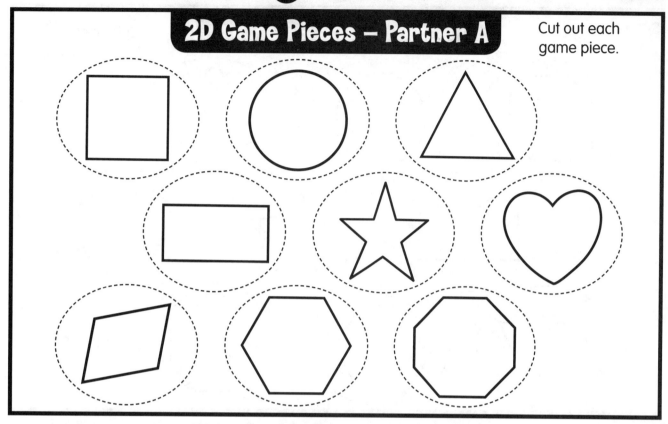

2D Game Pieces – Partner B

Cut out each game piece.

String Beads

3D Game Pieces – Partner A

Cut out each game piece.

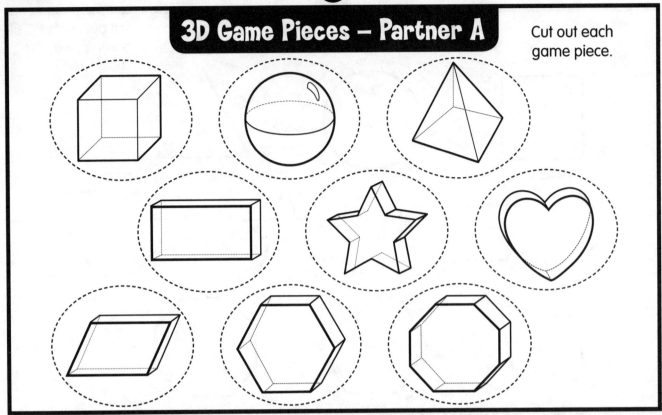

3D Game Pieces – Partner B

Cut out each game piece.

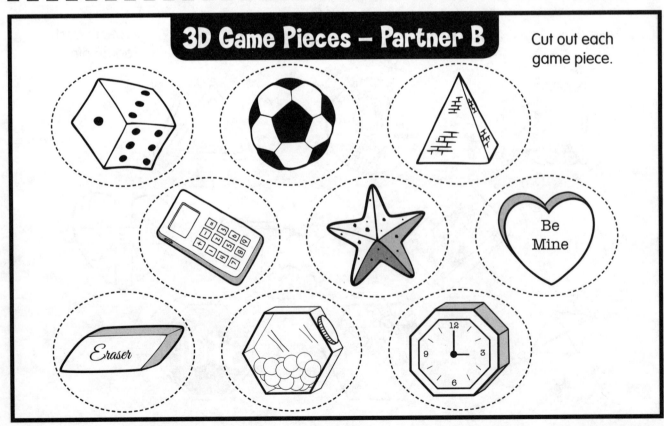

Match Mine: Primary
Kagan Publishing • 1 (800) 933-2667 • www.KaganOnline.com

Swamp Life

Partner A asks Partner B to find a specific animal on a lily pad game piece and tells Partner B where to place that animal on a lily pad on the Swamp Life game board. Partner B cooperates with Partner A to make a match.

Vocabulary

- Alligator
- Beaver
- Bottom
- Column
- Dragonfly
- Duck
- First
- Fish
- Frog
- Heron
- Last
- Lily pad
- Middle
- Next
- Row
- Second
- Snail
- Swamp
- Third
- Top
- Turtle

Game Board

Game Pieces

Common Core State Standards

MATH:
K.G.A.1 Describe objects in the environment using names of shapes, and describe the relative position of these objects using terms such as *above, below, beside, in front of, behind*, and *next to*.

SPEAKING & LISTENING:
COMPREHENSION AND COLLABORATION
SL.K.1a, SL.1.1a, SL.2.1a Follow agreed-upon rules for discussions.
SL.K.3, SL.1.3, SL.2.3 Ask and answer questions in order to seek help, get information, or clarify something that is not understood.

PRESENTATION OF KNOWLEDGE AND IDEAS
SL.K.6 Speak audibly and express thoughts, feelings, and ideas clearly.
SL.1.6, SL.2.6 Produce complete sentences when appropriate to task and situation.

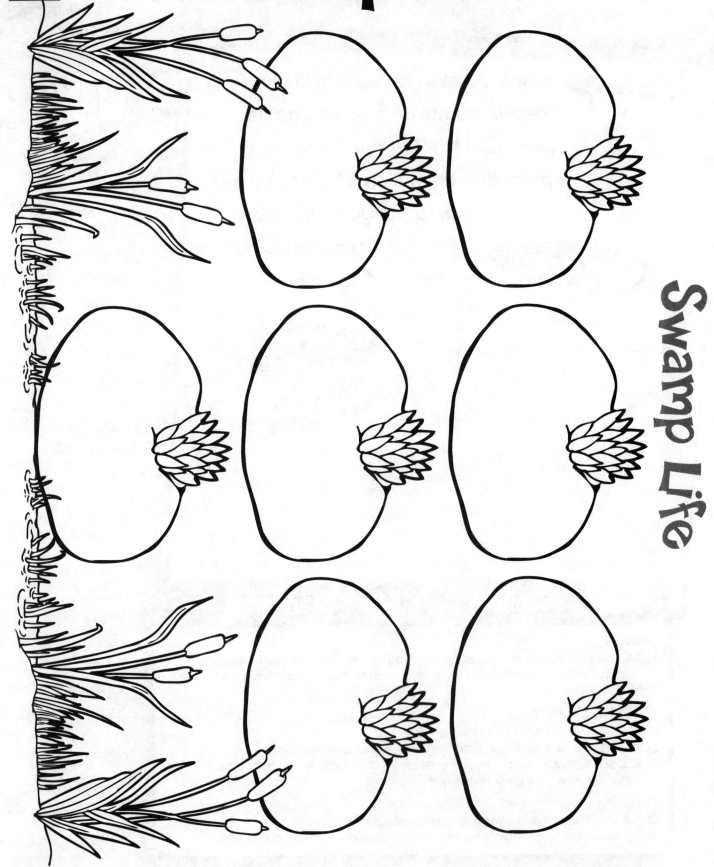

Swamp Life

Swamp Life

Game Pieces – Partner A

Cut out each
game piece.

Swamp Life

Game Pieces – Partner B

Cut out each
game piece.

Match Mine: Primary
Kagan Publishing • 1 (800) 933-2667 • www.KaganOnline.com

Partner A reads the homophone game piece and tells Partner B to find a corresponding homophone game piece and place it on the Treasure Chest game board.

Partner B cooperates with Partner A to make a match.

Game Board

Game Pieces

Homophone Matches

- Do–Due
- Bee–Be
- I–Eye
- Tale–Tail
- Blue–Blew
- Mail–Male
- Knight–Night
- Hair–Hare
- Buy–Bye
- So–Sew
- Sun–Bun
- Tee–Tea
- One–Won
- Deer–Dear
- Ate–Eight
- Bare–Bear
- There–Their
- Doe–Dough

Vocabulary

- Bottom
- Column
- Diamond
- First
- Fourth
- Gem
- Gold
- Heart
- Jewel
- Middle
- Oval
- Rectangle
- Rounded Octagon
- Row
- Second
- Square
- Tear drop
- Third
- Top
- Treasure chest
- Triangle

Common Core State Standards

MATH:
K.G.A.1 Describe objects in the environment using names of shapes, and describe the relative position of these objects using terms such as *above, below, beside, in front of, behind,* and *next to.*

SPEAKING & LISTENING:
COMPREHENSION AND COLLABORATION
SL.K.1a, SL.1.1a, SL.2.1a Follow agreed-upon rules for discussions.
SL.K.3, SL.1.3, SL.2.3 Ask and answer questions in order to seek help, get information, or clarify something that is not understood.

PRESENTATION OF KNOWLEDGE AND IDEAS
SL.K.6 Speak audibly and express thoughts, feelings, and ideas clearly.
SL.1.6, SL.2.6 Produce complete sentences when appropriate to task and situation.

Treasure Chest

Match Mine: Primary
Kagan Publishing • 1 (800) 933-2667 • www.KaganOnline.com

Treasure Chest

Game 27

Game Pieces – Partner A

Cut out each jewel.

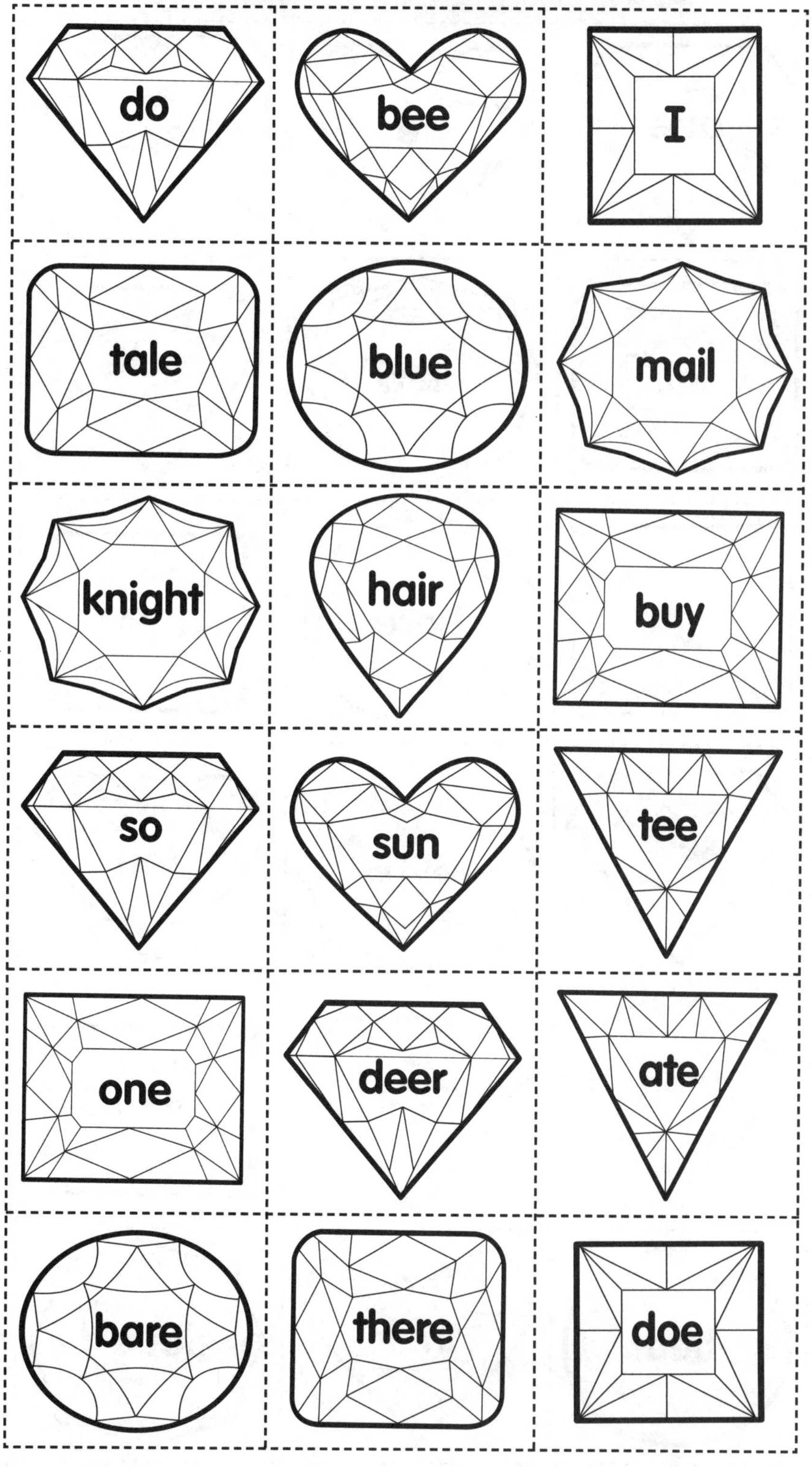
do
bee
I
tale
blue
mail
knight
hair
buy
so
sun
tee
one
deer
ate
bare
there
doe

Treasure Chest

Cut out each
game piece.

due	be	eye
tail	blew	male
night	hare	bye
sew	son	tea
won	dear	eight
bear	their	dough

Match Mine: Primary
Kagan Publishing • 1 (800) 933-2667 • www.KaganOnline.com

Weather Watchers

Game 28

Partner A asks Partner B to find a weather pattern game piece and tells Partner B where to place it on the Weather Watchers game board. Partner B cooperates with Partner A to make a match.

Game Board

Game 28 Weather Watchers

WEATHER WATCHERS

Game Pieces

Weather Watchers Game 28

Game Pieces – Partner A

Cut out each game piece.

Vocabulary

- Blizzard
- Cloudy
- Flood
- Foggy
- Freezing
- Hail
- Heatwave
- Hurricane
- Partly cloudy
- Rain
- Rainbow
- Raindrop
- Snow
- Snowflake
- Storm
- Sunny
- Tornado
- Windy

Common Core State Standards

MATH:
K.G.A.1 Describe objects in the environment using names of shapes, and describe the relative position of these objects using terms such as *above, below, beside, in front of, behind,* and *next to.*

SPEAKING & LISTENING:
COMPREHENSION AND COLLABORATION
SL.K.1a, SL.1.1a, SL.2.1a Follow agreed-upon rules for discussions.
SL.K.3, SL.1.3, SL.2.3 Ask and answer questions in order to seek help, get information, or clarify something that is not understood.

PRESENTATION OF KNOWLEDGE AND IDEAS
SL.K.6 Speak audibly and express thoughts, feelings, and ideas clearly.
SL.1.6, SL.2.6 Produce complete sentences when appropriate to task and situation.

Match Mine: Primary
Kagan Publishing • 1 (800) 933-2667 • www.KaganOnline.com

195

Weather Watchers

Match Mine: Primary
Kagan Publishing • 1 (800) 933-2667 • www.KaganOnline.com

Weather Watchers

Game Pieces – Partner A

Cut out each game piece.

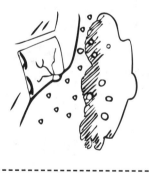   

Weather Watchers

Game Pieces – Partner B

Cut out each
game piece.

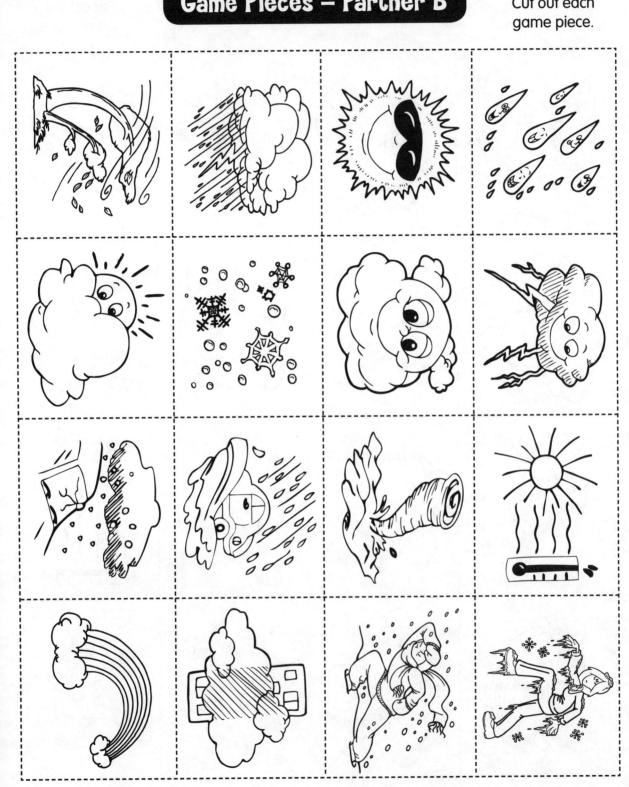

Match Mine: Primary
Kagan Publishing • 1 (800) 933-2667 • www.KaganOnline.com

Zim Zam Zip

Partner A sends one direction at a time, telling Partner B where to place the game pieces on the Zim Zam Zip game board. Partner B cooperates with Partner A to make a match.

Game Board

Zim Zam Zip

Game Pieces

Zim Zam Zip

Game Pieces – Partner A

Cut out each game piece.

Vocabulary

- Antenna
- Booties
- Circle
- Eyeballs
- Facing
- Forward
- Front
- Fuzzy
- Hairy
- Left
- Right
- Round
- Smile
- Stripes
- Triangle

Common Core State Standards

MATH:
K.G.A.1 Describe objects in the environment using names of shapes, and describe the relative position of these objects using terms such as *above, below, beside, in front of, behind,* and *next to.*

SPEAKING & LISTENING:
COMPREHENSION AND COLLABORATION
SL.K.1a, SL.1.1a, SL.2.1a Follow agreed-upon rules for discussions.
SL.K.3, SL.1.3, SL.2.3 Ask and answer questions in order to seek help, get information, or clarify something that is not understood.

PRESENTATION OF KNOWLEDGE AND IDEAS
SL.K.6 Speak audibly and express thoughts, feelings, and ideas clearly.
SL.1.6, SL.2.6 Produce complete sentences when appropriate to task and situation.

Zim Zam Zip

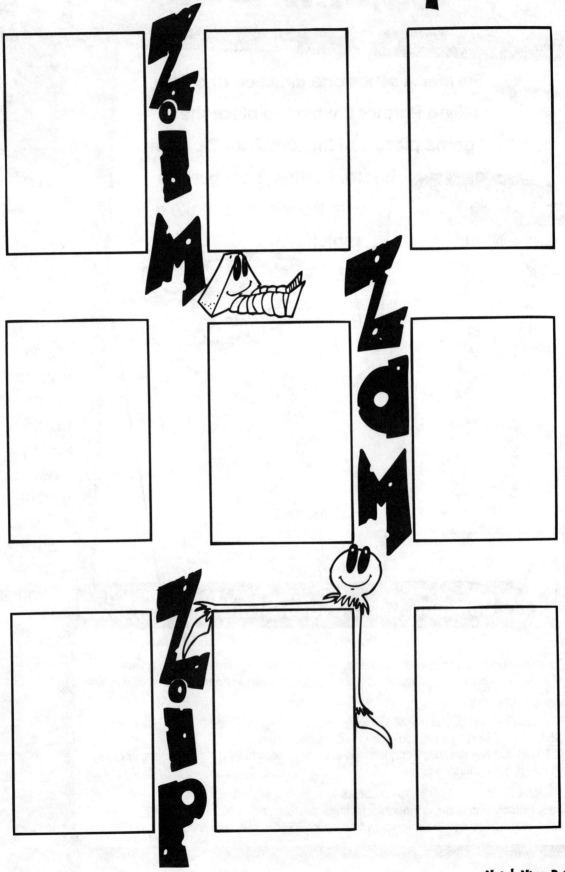

Match Mine: Primary
Kagan Publishing • 1 (800) 933-2667 • www.KaganOnline.com

Zim Zam Zip

Game Pieces – Partner A

Cut out each
game piece.

Zim Zam Zip

Game Pieces – Partner B

Cut out each
game piece.

Match Mine: Primary
Kagan Publishing • 1 (800) 933-2667 • www.KaganOnline.com

Partner A sends one direction at a time, telling Partner B where to place the Zoo Animal game pieces on the Zoo Animals game board. Partner B cooperates with Partner A to make a match.

Game Board

Game Pieces

Vocabulary

- Alligator
- Bottom
- Cheetah
- Elephant
- First
- Flag
- Flamingo
- Fourth
- Giraffe
- Hippo
- Last
- Monkey
- Penguin
- Polar bear
- Prairie dog
- Rhino
- Seal
- Second
- Sloth
- Snake
- Third
- Tiger
- Top
- Turtle
- Walrus
- Zebra

Common Core State Standards

MATH:
K.G.A.1 Describe objects in the environment using names of shapes, and describe the relative position of these objects using terms such as *above, below, beside, in front of, behind,* and *next to.*

SPEAKING & LISTENING:
COMPREHENSION AND COLLABORATION
SL.K.1a, SL.1.1a, SL.2.1a Follow agreed-upon rules for discussions.
SL.K.3, SL.1.3, SL.2.3 Ask and answer questions in order to seek help, get information, or clarify something that is not understood.

PRESENTATION OF KNOWLEDGE AND IDEAS
SL.K.6 Speak audibly and express thoughts, feelings, and ideas clearly.
SL.1.6, SL.2.6 Produce complete sentences when appropriate to task and situation.

Zoo Animals

Match Mine: Primary

Kagan Publishing • 1 (800) 933-2667 • www.KaganOnline.com

Zoo Animals

Game
30

Game Pieces – Partner A

Cut out each
game piece.

Zoo Animals

Game Pieces – Partner B

Cut out each
game piece.

Match Mine: Primary
Kagan Publishing • 1 (800) 933-2667 • www.KaganOnline.com